What people are saying about

The Truth Inside

Ali has endured the hardest of losses and she's not only surviving but is thriving. Authentic and real, this beautiful book of hope for us all not only touches the heart but opens the mind to a greater reality where love never dies. A wonderful read which speaks to the true healing potential of mediumship. Romy will be proud.
Claire Broad, bestselling co-author, *Answers from Heaven*

Ali's book radiates her belief of life after life. She provides within her book examples that show that a connection, both seen and unseen, still exists after a loved one dies.

Her words are a gift to all those who mourn the loss of a loved one whether a child, parent or beloved other.
Angie Buxton-King, author, *The NHS Healer*

A remarkable story of love overcoming grief and the awakening of a soul to a higher purpose. I am certain that this book was sent from the heavens.
Gordon Smith, hailed as The UK's most accurate medium

Ali Norell has posted several beautiful features with great success and feedback on my popular Facebook author page. She writes with heart and soul and her story is a healing, comforting and truly inspiring book just waiting to happen.
Theresa Cheung, *Sunday Times* Top 10 bestselling author

T0158663

The Truth Inside

Lessons From My Daughter In The Afterlife

The Truth Inside

Lessons From My Daughter In The Afterlife

Ali Norell

BOOKS

Winchester, UK
Washington, USA

First published by O-Books, 2019
O-Books is an imprint of John Hunt Publishing Ltd., 3 East St., Alresford,
Hampshire SO24 9EE, UK
office1@jhpbooks.net
www.johnhuntpublishing.com

For distributor details and how to order please visit the 'Ordering' section on our website.

Text copyright: Ali Norell 2018

ISBN: 978 1 78535 572 1
978 1 78535 837 1 (ebook)
Library of Congress Control Number: 2018934960

A CIP catalogue record for this book is available from the British Library.

Design: Stuart Davies

UK: Printed and bound by CPI Group (UK) Ltd, Croydon, CR0 4YY
US: Printed and bound by Thomson Shore, 7300 West Joy Road, Dexter, MI 48130

We operate a distinctive and ethical publishing philosophy in
all areas of our business, from our global network of authors to
production and worldwide distribution.

Contents

Romy Silvia Satya Norell
26th March – 18th July 2014

For Romy.

And for Kasper, Layla, Macsen and Darius.

"No coming, no going."

Introduction

I began writing this book as homage to my daughter Romy. I hoped that it would honour her brief existence with us and soothe my grief. However, realising the true purpose of this book – all that it means to me and all that I hope it will mean to others – has been a journey of epic proportions. During the writing of it I came to learn a lot about my "new" self and to fully appreciate my purpose in this lifetime. I owe a huge debt of gratitude to Romy because if she had not died, I would not be living my life in such a purposeful and vibrant way. If I tell you that I truly believe that, at some level, not only did I know that my daughter was not meant to stay long in this life, but that in some way she and I planned it in advance of coming to our lives here on earth, then you may find your thinking about life, death and everything in between to be challenged.

From the outset I was determined that this book would not be what is sometimes referred to as "misery lit". Even after I lost my own child, I did not want to read stories of other people's children passing to Spirit. I didn't want to read of other people's grief. Neither could I imagine why anyone would genuinely want to read of mine, other than out of loyalty or some kind of ghoulish curiosity. I knew that Romy's story formed part of what I needed to tell but I wanted my book to have a clear purpose: to help others in some way. I am not a bereavement counsellor; in fact I wasn't even a particularly good recipient of it myself. In the months following my daughter's death I searched high and low for something meaningful that could ease my pain and also bring some element of joy and positivity back into my life and as much as I tried to deviate, the roads all led me back to one thing: Spiritualism, and the belief in some kind of existence after what we call death.

Throughout my life I have been aware of an ability. For as

long as I can remember I have been able to see, hear and sense energies (referred to as being psychic) and communicate with the spirits of people who have died (this is known as mediumship). I'm careful not to call it a gift because this doesn't sit well with me. To me, a gift is the ability to create or produce something of beauty or worth, sometimes with very little effort; it comes naturally. In some ways my ability does come naturally, but I have also dedicated many years to developing it. For the most part, I pursued this because it inspired me and because I enjoyed being in the company of other like-minded individuals. I was happy working as a reflexologist and a healer and doing the odd sitting for friends and acquaintances but in no way did I ever imagine myself working as a fully-fledged psychic medium. Despite being a confident, self-assured person I was very afraid of recognising this part of myself and above all of admitting it to others. I worried that people's perceptions of me would not be kind and that I would be ridiculed for my beliefs and my abilities. Of course, hundreds of years ago my fear would have had a very real basis because mediums, psychics, readers and seers were all relentlessly persecuted by an establishment who felt threatened by the empowerment that these individuals could pass on to so-called ordinary people.

These days, some mediums call themselves "intuitive coaches" and give trusted advice and direction to people in positions of authority all over the world but still some of us keep to the shadows; afraid to step forward and live our own truth fully. In short, I spent most of my early adult life studying and developing my mediumship skills purely for my own fulfilment while living in denial that I could use this ability for the benefit of others, and to serve Spirit. Alongside this extracurricular activity I worked in a series of "careers": as a receptionist, a PA, a multilingual tour guide and as a public relations manager. Little did I realise then but these jobs were a great preparation for this phase of my life.

When I look back at those professions now I can clearly see that they all had one thing in common: communication. I am a communicator, and the experience I gained in these situations during my twenties and thirties has prepared me very well for the business of communicating with Spirit and translating the messages they give me into relatable information for the people who need and request it.

It has not been an easy trajectory. Losing my own child shook and challenged my spiritual beliefs to the core and I did my very best to turn my back on them as I tried desperately to cling on to my sanity, my surviving children and my life. When I say that I "knew" Romy was not meant to stay with us, this is not a cut and dried statement. It's very difficult to explain but from the moment I knew I was pregnant right up until she lost consciousness that day I would have said I had no inkling that I wasn't going to watch her grow up with me. However, as soon as the events of 17th July 2014 began to unfold I experienced what I can only describe as an inner knowing. Even in the midst of the unspeakable trauma of losing my child I felt a sense that this was something I had seen coming in some way I couldn't fathom.

That didn't stop me from feeling all the usual emotions attached to the grieving process. Anger, guilt, devastation, suicidal thoughts: I had them all. If anyone acted on the ill-conceived idea to start any kind of spiritual conversation with me I had to carefully remind myself not to respond aggressively. Apart from my husband Darius and our immediate family members, I couldn't bring myself to engage in any kind of conversation about what had happened or why. I was consumed with anger and hopelessness. Why had this happened to us? I didn't care about the spirit world, I just wanted my daughter back and I was beside myself knowing that this wasn't going to happen.

Several months after Romy died, I began to experience the kind of communication that I had always had with Spirit, but this time it came from my own baby daughter. I tested my theories over and over: how could a baby so young communicate with me from the spirit world? Was she growing up on "the other side"? What could she be trying to tell me? Not trusting my own abilities, I sought the help and advice of several established mediums. I saw a handful of them privately in one-to-one sittings and I began to frequent my local Spiritualist church every week, when a different medium would take to the platform and deliver messages to those of us in the congregation. On many occasions these messages were directed at me.

As the experiences and messages began to mount up I started to see that I was amassing a collection that pointed to the undeniable fact (for me) that my daughter's spirit continued on in some way. If I were merely recounting my own experiences I could forgive you for thinking that you were listening to the ramblings of a grief-stricken mother. If I told you that a medium had given me a message then the sceptical could find grounds to discount it, I'm sure. However, I can cross-reference numerous personal experiences with information from one-to-one sittings and messages from mediums on platforms who have never met me before. I even received a remote message from a medium via a friend. She had attended a sitting on the day of Romy's remembrance service and was shocked when the medium not only told her that she had come from a child's memorial but also spelled out Romy's name correctly and gave further information known to me, but not to my friend.

Ironically, these experiences from beyond the grave started to bring me back to life. After initially turning away, I began to rediscover my faith in Spiritualism and eventually found my way back to a development circle. I now know that I do have a purpose with this work and am looking forward to establishing myself as a working medium.

During a conversation over morning coffee one day with my husband I made an impulsive decision to begin writing a blog about my experience. I wasn't brave enough to include a focus on Spiritualism at that point but I was clear that I wanted to offer a truthful account of my experience that might in turn give direction and hope to other bereaved parents, something to counteract the outpourings of anger, grief and desperation I had found in online support forums. It shocked me to find that, within these safe online spaces for those mourning a child or children, there seemed to be no peace and very little positivity. Parents who had lost children years previously still seemed to be in the same state of horrified disbelief that had begun to accompany them on their bereavement journey. I didn't want this. I knew that if I was going to survive the experience, fulfil my marriage commitments and be a good mother to my two (later, three) surviving children I had to find a way to give myself positivity and hope for the future or my spirit would quite literally die, even if my body did not. What began as a blog to help me to process my grief served to remind me that I had always dreamed of being a writer. Mindful that I needed to reconcile this time in my life as somehow "part of the plan" I began to ask Spirit for guidance. Within a few short months a series of apparent coincidences saw me attend a writer's workshop, which in turn produced a book proposal and several chapters and, before I knew it, a publishing deal.

I know with absolutely certainty that Spirit – and Romy – always intended for me to do this work. I am an ordinary person to whom the extraordinary has happened. To many, this "extraordinary" may appear to be an unimaginable nightmare but I would like to show you how my return to my belief in the afterlife and the spirit world not only eased my grief but also shaped the entire course of my life going forward. Many books exist charting how writers survive tragedy to become stronger but what if these so-called tragedies are pre-planned by us? What if we plan exactly what we need to learn from them to move forward with purpose in our life? What if tragedy is meant to be embraced rather than survived? My experiences have proved to me beyond doubt that we are all born with a deep, inherent knowledge of our purpose; why we are here. We all know someone who just seems to step lightly into a particular job or lifestyle; as if they were born to it. They take to it like a duck to water and quietly carry on about their business. Some of us just need bigger prompts to recall our purpose than others and this might be part of the lesson we have chosen to learn while we're here.

How I Hope You Will Use This Book

Personally, I don't like to pick up a book that I think tells a great story only to find that story peppered with stops, starts and interruptions from well-meaning exercises, visualisations and meditations. To my mind, an instruction manual is an instruction manual is an instruction manual. However, I also feel strangely satisfied if I feel I have taken away some kind of insight or inspiration from a book. If I get absorbed in a story it often feels like a chore to comb back through what I have read to try and gauge a deeper meaning from it. By placing prompts at the end of each chapter I hope that they will help you to assimilate what you have read. When I help my children with their school reading I ask them questions about the pages they've read that night and feel slightly dismayed at how little they appear to have remembered. Then I try the technique on myself and get a shock when I see how little information I myself have retained after just half an hour of reading.

Today's world is so geared to short, sharp bursts of information – social media sites, sound bites, fast food, ever faster Internet connection, electronic reading devices and multitasking – that our brains seem to have lost the capacity to absorb a stream of information and then regurgitate it. So the prompts are a way of checking in, of inviting you to chew over what you've read and make it relevant by applying it to your own life. Perhaps they might also serve as writing prompts for journals or a springboard for discussion in a book club.

My hope is that they will also help you to look at my story and the ideas I have applied to help myself and relate them to your own life situations. You'll see that I'm nobody special. I am not in possession of a mystical gift; I just listen and look at events in my life in a certain way. Yes, I communicate with Spirit but I have spent many years of my life studying to learn how to develop this ability. We all of us have the ability to recognise signs from Spirit and once we stop telling ourselves to stop being ridiculous we might find that these signs are more prescient than we think. Try adopting this perspective for a short time and see what this brings for you.

Anyone can learn to look at all that life has to offer in a positive light. I'm not suggesting that you have to "believe" – in Spiritualism or anything else – in order to do so, but if you can find a way to understand that perhaps whatever you are doing in your life is what you have decided to do on one level or another, I promise you that your life will begin to feel less arduous. By using the prompts in this way I hope that my story garners more recognition for being purposeful than merely an inspirational read. I do not feel inspiring. I still have days when I feel as if I can't get out of bed. I shout at my children, I am irritable with my husband and I have moments when I honestly can't see the point of it all. Since encountering my spirit guides, I do feel an invisible pair of hands at work in these moments; steadying my shoulders and quietly willing me on. Coincidentally or not, I am a much more positive person these days.

This is not an instruction manual for self-improvement or mastery of mediumship, and it does not tell you how to survive and thrive after trauma. It encourages you to consider the idea that whatever difficulties you are facing in your life right now, you have asked for. I don't mean that you have quite literally done so in the colloquial sense; I mean that you planned it, in the Spirit world, before you were born here and you planned it because there was something you intended to learn from it. If we do not come to this life to learn, then what is the point? Life is not to be survived, it is to be lived.

I believe that we choose to incarnate and live our lives with a specific group of souls. Some of these souls are put in our path to challenge, or even to hurt us. Some are present to nurture and support us, and some are players in the scene of our lives; replaying themes from previous incarnations to help us to achieve our spiritual potential. However, our entrance and our exit as a soul are made entirely alone. Even twins cannot physically journey down the birth canal at the same time; one has to come before the other. I spent over a decade studying birth as a reflexologist, birth doula and healer and looking back at those years now I fully appreciate that this was not a random choice on my part. In fact, during my training as a reflexologist we had to choose a specialist topic to study and I was torn between working with birth and death. Even at that point in my life I recognised that the line between these two states is thin.

From all those years in the privileged position of accompanying women as they birthed their babies and having now birthed four of my own I can assert that the journey of being born is much harder than that of dying. And yet, our society insists on seeing birth as positive and death as something to be feared. Both are events that ultimately we must actively experience alone. There may be people around us to assist, but the first and the final steps are ours to take; they are part of our blueprint, of what makes us uniquely ourselves. The ensuing years in which we play out our story are time in which we can, if we wish, learn to uncover and live our own truth.

Acknowledgements

My wish is to acknowledge each and every person who has touched my life, from early inspiration to my development as a medium and an author to the love and support I received following Romy's passing. This is impossible, so if you do not find your name written here please know that it is written in my heart. You all know who you are.

Firstly I would like to thank my publisher, John Hunt Publishing, for taking a chance on an unknown author and helping me to get this book out into the world. I am both touched by and grateful for your belief in my work and commitment to helping it realise its potential. John Hunt, Dominic James, Maria Barry, Elizabeth Radley, Beccy Conway, Mary Flatt, Nick Welch, Stuart Davies and Trevor Greenfield: thank you for your sensitivity in working with my words and your brilliance in adapting images for a truly meaningful cover design. I would also like to thank my dear friend and mentor Theresa Cheung for her gracious and generous support and for her many superb books, which have inspired and comforted me, both before and after Romy's passing. My thanks also to Claire Broad for her support and encouragement.

I thank from my heart Gerrie March and Dorothy Young, two exceptional mediums who have been instrumental in helping me to develop my abilities. Thank you also to the other members of our Brighton Circle whose warmth has lifted me and carried me forward. I would also like to recognise the work of Gordon Smith, a kind soul and inspirational medium who has used his exceptional abilities to bring relief and understanding to many bereaved parents.

Of the many amazing people I am fortunate to call friends, a small number I have to mention by name as their support has helped me in shaping this book. Thank you, Natasha

Merchant, for patiently attending Spiritualist churches with me, for your beautiful photography and persistence at being my friend during the most difficult days. Thank you, Em Myers, for your loyalty, for encouraging me to move forwards with my mediumship and for your amazing cakes. Heartfelt thanks to two dear friends: Jennifer Plenty for such constant support and for always remembering Romy in such small but significant ways and Suzanne Mark for your friendship from the first days of our arrival in Sussex. To the entire Dharma Primary School community for welcoming our family and enveloping us in your warmth when we so needed it. Thank you, Jeannette Adair, for sharing such personal memories and for listening so well over lots of cups of tea. Thank you, Karla Courtney and Celina Lucas, for your time and input into my first book proposal. To Leslie Mallman, my thanks for your enduring friendship across many years, thousands of miles and countless slices of chocolate cake. You are a reliable sounding board and I am so thankful for your friendship.

I must thank Bill Kistler, my friend and mentor, for all the opportunities you gave me in the world of work and for showing me by example that generosity of spirit towards those around you is always the way to go. Your photograph of me with Romy is among my most treasured possessions and it is a privilege to call you and Ulli my friends.

To Melanie Sanders: thank you for going above and beyond and for giving your wonderful friendship and love to our whole family, especially during my fourth pregnancy. Although you never made it to a birth, you have always been with me in spirit and your positivity and belief in me carried me through. To Helen Piper, for encouraging me with the blog which eventually became the seed of inspiration for this book, for driving six hours in one day just to sit with me for an afternoon when I needed you and for still being my friend even though you think my outlook on life is weird.

Acknowledgements

To Michelle Ramiro and Emma Round, for their lifetime (in fact I am sure this is many lifetimes) of friendship. There are so many things I could thank you both for; most of all for always knowing what I am thinking without my having to explain anything. I marvel at how we have grown together over forty years of friendship despite distance and challenges. You are family and our bond is unique. I can always, always rely on you both to be late for anything.

It goes without saying that I have much to thank my family for. I consider myself truly blessed to call Suzanne Norell and Nuria Kruger my mother-in-law and sister-in-law. Thank you both, so much, for your enduring love and encouragement during the writing of this book and for being so willing to embrace my interest in Spiritualism and healing. Suzanne, thank you especially for flying over from Spain to look after our children while I wrote, and Nuria, thank you for setting up the blog that became such a lifeline to me in my darkest time and for giving such helpful feedback on the first draft of my proposal for this book. The cheerleading you have both given me from afar has helped me more than I can say.

I would also like to use this opportunity to give my love and thanks to my two wonderful brothers-in-law, Rory McGauran and Les Kruger. Thank you for your quiet support over many years, and for always being there when needed. My love goes to all our wonderful nephews and to our niece: Ryan, Luke, Elliott, Julian and Stella.

I would like to give special thanks to my aunt, Sue Fulling; one of the few people to really know exactly what I have been through. It has helped me beyond words to know that you were always on hand to listen right from the first hours after Romy passed. This book is also for you, for Ken and for Nicola, with my love.

To my parents, Ray and Viv Cuthbert, and my sister Claire McGauran: thank you all for always having my back and for listening to and supporting me without judgement. Mum and Dad, thank you for buying me my first typewriter and, many years later, the laptop on which this book was written, for encouraging my writing as a child and for bringing me up to be open to the spirit world. On a practical note, thank you also for your hours of childcare that have enabled me to write. Claire, thank you for your loyalty. However hard things have got in my life I have always known that I can rely on you without question and this is truly special. Thank you for being there for Romy, and for us, during her last hours with us. Thank you for celebrating our differences, for never being afraid to tell it how it is and for all the times we have rendered ourselves helpless with laughter.

In line with the subject matter of this book I must also thank all my guides, helpers and loved ones in Spirit. I thank my guide, Xian, for his patience and understanding as I conquered my fears and all the guides I feel standing in the background, ready to come forward and help me in my mediumship and my life. In particular I give thanks to Noory and Jeannette Norell and all four of my grandparents – Stuart and Sylvia Cuthbert and Bert and Eleanor Fulling – whose love and encouragement I have felt throughout my life, from this world and the next.

Thank you to Kasper, Layla and Macsen for choosing me as your Mama. Your own individual gifts make you a joy to be around and you have been my inspiration to keep going at times when I have felt I couldn't. Thank you, Romy, for all that you shared and continue to share with me.

My final thanks have to go to my husband, Darius Norell: the north to my south and the air to my fire. The things I have to thank you for are countless, but the most special are the four amazing children we created together. Thank you for always wanting to give me the world, for walking beside me even when I could not stand, and most of all for always encouraging me to follow my dreams. This book would not exist without your love.

Prologue

I once was blind but now I see.

– Warr Acres, Hymn of Remembrance

17th July 2014 was a blisteringly hot day in West Sussex, a rural county around 40 miles south of London, close to the large British seaside town of Brighton.

On that day, I sent an email to my husband, Darius, from my phone as I sat in a charming café in our neighbouring village with our youngest daughter Romy, four-and-a-half-months old. We had dropped her older brother and sister – Kasper and Layla, then aged five and four – off at school and nursery on foot before the heat of the day set in and returned home to pick up the car. It was the last day before the schools broke for the long summer holiday and we were seriously considering a move to the next village along. As I accelerated the car up the steep incline of our road I started chatting to Romy, as was my habit. "Well, Romy," I said, "this is our last day together." I was referring to the fact that the following day we would be joined by her siblings and the glorious disarray of the summer holidays would begin.

This felt like a time of vast and imminent change for our family. After relocating from London to a small Sussex village five years previously, we had enjoyed our time there but both Darius and I felt as if something didn't quite fit. Now a family of five, we wanted to gain a little more floor space and move closer to Brighton, the large seaside town we felt had so much to offer both ourselves and our growing children. We had taken Romy on a recce a week or so previously and seen a large, ramshackle property we couldn't quite afford. Undeterred by the fact that it needed some work doing to it, we had spent the previous evening talking through various options and costs and were considering putting in an offer. As part of our grand moving plan I had decided to drive over and explore the village properly with Romy to see if it felt right; if I could see us living there. For obvious reasons I felt reluctant to take all three children on this mission, so today was the day.

I sat at the back table in the café, which adjoined a flower shop owned by the same business. I felt myself relaxing into my seat away from the heat of the day, which at 10:30am was already stifling. I couldn't tear my eyes away from the adjacent florist, full of vibrancy and colour, bursting with the intoxicating scent and promise of summer days, and from this vantage point I could see all the other customers coming and going. Strangely for such a beautiful summer morning, there were very few other customers seated with us. Most popped in for a takeaway coffee and a croissant and left again. I ordered mushrooms on toast – a dish now etched on to my memory as evocative of that particular day – and laughed as I tried to eat it with Romy on my lap. I was still breastfeeding and we hadn't started weaning, though in typically over-organised fashion I had already gone and bought all the little pots, curvy spoons and paraphernalia as I was so looking forward to seeing which foods she would enjoy. Sitting on my lap, she was already grasping for the fork and I wondered whether she might share my love of mushrooms.

That morning is forever freeze-framed in my mind. Nowhere to be, nowhere to go. Full of anticipation and hope for our family's future, I really did sit back in my seat and thank the stars for my good fortune. I felt a sudden surge of excitement and optimism and wanted to share my feeling with Darius. I haphazardly typed an email one-handed while trying to keep the pronged end of the fork away from Romy's face. It read: "We're sitting in a gorgeous café, the village is lovely. I think we'd all be really happy here. Let's do it! Xxx".

I made up my mind that I would contact the estate agent when I got home and set the necessary chain of events in motion for us to make the move. We had always made these types of decisions impulsively – mainly thanks to me and my intuition – and my sense told me that transformative change was coming for us. As it turned out I was right about the change but I really had no idea of the devastation we would experience before that transformation occurred.

Time stood still for a while in that place and every time I think of it I am so glad it did. I sang to my daughter, gave her endless kisses and we laughed together. At around 11:30 I realised that I hadn't fed Romy, which was unusual as she was a big baby and always happy to feed. I was also concerned about getting her to drink more fluids as the weather had been so uncomfortably hot. I settled her to feed but she refused it – something she had never done before and which caused me to feel mildly concerned.

Sensing that she was getting a little restless, I decided that perhaps the heat was making her feel tired. I put her down in her pram, organised my bags and made ready to leave. I thought it would be best to drive back home, sit quietly in the cool of our living room and try feeding her again there. I figured she would probably fall asleep in the car on the way home. Just as we were leaving, she did something else I had never seen her do: she let out a really loud scream and started to cry. I hastily picked her up to comfort her and felt perplexed. This was so unlike Romy, she was such a sunny-natured, easy-going baby. I began to feel a pressing need to get her home.

Holding her seemed to have calmed her and she had slipped into sleep, so I put her down in the pram again and set off for the car park. I kept a close eye on her as we walked and she seemed unusually restless, which I tried to convince myself was down to the heat. We stopped briefly in the local supermarket to buy water and headed for the car park. Romy did indeed sleep all the way home.

Little more than 24 hours later, she was dead.

Following exhaustive tests, scans and discussions, we were told that the cause of Romy's death would always be unclear. The most comprehensive suggestion was that it was a type of cerebral aneurysm leading to brain haemorrhage. It was impossible to gain a definitive conclusion from any of the scans as the bleed to her brain had been so sudden, so fast and so overwhelming that the source could not be pinpointed.

I lost many things when Romy left us. My identity changed forever. I was no longer the positive, optimistic, driven woman I had been. The complacent belief that nothing really bad would ever happen to me lay in pieces. I became not just a mother but a bereaved mother which is, as I was later to discover, a heavy title to carry. I lost my dream of a big family, of having two daughters near enough together in age to be close as sisters, as I am with my sister. I lost sight of my future because I could not bear to imagine it without Romy, and also because I developed a deep-seated fear that other things were going to happen to us with which I would not be able to cope. As a mother, I am also ashamed to admit that I contemplated ending my own life, although it was always the thought of my surviving children that pulled me back from the brink. I could not make sense of anything which decreed that my daughter could be "taken from me" in such a brutal manner and I blamed myself for not being able to save her. I lost my world as I knew it, I lost my spiritual perspective and I damn near lost my mind; but I did, over time, find my truth.

The story I want to tell you is not one of enlightenment or of triumph over adversity because I do not feel as if I have triumphed over anything, nor do I believe that we should look at the death of loved ones and the ensuing grief as something to be overcome. I still struggle with my grief. I still live with Post Traumatic Stress Disorder and depression. However, I do know that having this experience has caused me to look at the world very differently. It has also led me back to beliefs I have always held but gave less importance to as time went on – that there is life after death and that we choose what we need to experience in this lifetime in order to learn – and I have found them reinforced. Thanks to events that began to unfold after Romy died, I have returned to developing the psychic and mediumistic abilities I have always possessed but been too fearful to truly admit to. I have uncovered my true self.

By looking for these clues from Spirit – so often given to me by Romy herself – I learned that my purpose in life is to write and to serve as a medium and a healer. Following this truth has led to my husband and I making many changes in our personal lives and taking decisions for our family that we might not have otherwise done. Uncovering my own truth has led to my writing this book.

This is my truth; and the story I want to tell you is how the death of my daughter led me to it. We all have our own truth; it is inside us. What is it? The answer to the question that nags at all human beings: "Why am I here?" We can seek it in spiritual practice, in the pages of books and the experiences of others but ultimately, and very simply, we are born knowing our own truth and if we learn to recognise the signs that Spirit/The Universe/ God/insert your own term here place in front of us then answers begin to be revealed.

It was only as I came to write this book – which I promised Romy I would do as I sat with her during the long, unbearable night of 17ᵗʰ July 2014 – that I realised that if she really was the embodiment of the Sanskrit middle name we gave her – Satya, meaning truth – then the truth really had been inside me all along.

This book is the story of how I literally gave birth to my truth. In reading it, I hope that you will begin to remember yours.

Chapter 1

The Truth

This above all: to thine own self be true.
– Shakespeare's *Hamlet*, Act 1, Scene 3

We are all seeking The Truth. But are we seeking the same truth? What is the truth? Those of us who consider ourselves to be spiritual seekers are endlessly searching for authenticity, a spiritual awakening, something that will confirm to us that there is more to life than... well, merely life. Even those who are not of a spiritual disposition are in search of truth. They find it in scientific progress, in practical answers to questions. They may ask, "How best may I live my life, because I only get one shot at it?"

I was brought up in an open-minded family wherein psychic abilities and belief in an afterlife were considered normal, so it was pretty inevitable that I would end up in the category of "spiritual seeker". I also believe that we only get one shot at life – this life, that is. I am of the belief that our souls exist outside of the physical body and that they experience many lifetimes. The purpose of one particular lifetime is to live, in practice, what we have set out for ourselves before we incarnate and to learn as much as possible. Sounds simple, right? It is. We tend to overcomplicate things in our human experience; so much so that we struggle to see what we have set out for ourselves to learn.

I believe that before we are born into this life we make a plan, or blueprint. We decide, with members of our soul group and other ascended souls, what it is that we wish to learn in this lifetime and how we will achieve it before we return to Spirit. We may actively decide to experience incredible hardship and difficulty; this is because the learning in these situations is greater. If life on earth is a classroom, what's the point in showing up to doodle on a piece of paper? If you want to extract the most from your experience, you have to work to the limits of your ability and sit the exam. As this book unfolds I will share with you how I came to remember and recognise my plan.

This may not be such an easy idea to accept but I can tell you that after years of grief, desperation and soul searching, this is the conclusion I have reached. What's more, the minute I decided to accept the idea that I had chosen to experience the loss of a child and the associated trauma, my life took a turn for the better. Without a moment's hesitation, I switched my life purpose from working with birth to helping others to understand death – strangely, a prediction I had made just weeks before Romy died. I realised a childhood dream of writing a book and I finally accepted that it was time to put my decade of mediumship training into practice. I felt as if layers of confusion had peeled away and I was left looking at: myself.

Likewise my husband, Darius, went from years of not quite feeling satisfied with his work to striking out on his own and following a deeper sense of how and with whom he should be working. From the offset, he found clients and organisations eager to work with him – and this after years of highs and lows and plans that never came fully to fruition.

The irony is not lost on either of us that we have created a dream existence, as individuals and for our family, with one staggeringly obvious omission: our youngest daughter is missing from the picture. Of course, we would give up everything in an instant to have her back with us but I do not believe that this would ever have been possible, just as I don't believe that we would be following this path had Romy not spent her short life with us before passing to Spirit. I am open to any practical suggestions to explain why we experienced this powerful shift after the death of our daughter but what I truly believe is that her passing allowed us to reconnect to a part of ourselves that we were fearful of seeing before. She somehow allowed us to see our truth.

In an additional twist which proves to me that we had some precognitive sense of what her purpose would be, we gave to our youngest daughter a middle name with exactly this meaning: Satya. We gave all four of our children a first name, a middle name and a second middle name derived from a Sanskrit word. We always thought that this third name would be largely ignored – both by our children and others – but that having it would bind the siblings together. This led to some lengthy discussions between us during which we questioned our sanity at choosing such a long string of unusual names for our offspring, but it felt important to do this. We wanted each of our children to revel in their own individuality and gave them names we hoped would reflect their strengths in life.

We fashioned Kasper out of two different spellings ("Kaspar" and "Casper"). In a nod to Darius's Persian heritage we gave to our son the name of a king, like that of his father. Kasper's Sanskrit name is Rohan, meaning "healing". Sure enough, our eldest son is a complex, highly sensitive and brilliantly engaging individual and parenting him has provided some truly healing moments for us all. Layla – born at a time when a hurricane of the same name ripped through Pakistan, and embodying this by arriving in 45 minutes flat – was a name I had always known I would give a daughter. The Sanskrit name we gave her is Shanti, meaning "peace". Layla is very often the peacemaker in our family and her kindness knows no bounds. After Romy came Macsen, named for a Welsh king, Macsen Wledig, in reference to my heritage. We spent a long time looking for his Sanskrit name but we eventually settled on Karuna, meaning "kindness and compassion for those who suffer". We regard all four of our children as blessings, but Macsen, coming as he did little more than a year after Romy left us, has truly been a salve to our terrible wounds of grief. He has eased my suffering in many ways, both large and small.

Romy's name began as a puzzle. I was standing in the kitchen one evening when I clearly heard a voice saying something that sounded like "Romany". I rushed to look up names with this sound and found Romy, a derivative of rosemary (a plant symbolic of remembrance) and meaning "dew of the sea". Despite never having heard of it before I knew without question that this was our daughter's name. We gave Romy the Sanskrit name Satya, meaning "truth". In all honesty, we thought we had chosen it because we liked the sound of it and it fit well with the names Romy and Silvia (for my grandmother) but we had no idea how prescient our choice was to be. For us, Romy came to symbolise the importance of living our truth. In particular for me, knowing the truth of what I came here to learn became overwhelmingly important. As I took steps to uncover this I started to recognise that I had known it all along. It was not seeking I needed to undertake, but remembering.

Going into my thirties I devoted a lot of time to developing my psychic and mediumistic abilities. I attended courses, workshops and demonstrations on every spiritual topic you could possibly imagine and I opened myself up to the spirit world. For years, I attended circle with the wonderful Gerrie March at the College of Psychic Studies in London, honing my skills and soaking up Gerrie's knowledge gained from many years as a professional medium. It was also something of a relief and a revelation to spend two hours each week in the company of like-minded individuals, all keen to develop their spiritual knowledge in order to help others and serve Spirit. The group got me through many ups and downs at that point in my life; always encouraging, always positive, welcoming and kind.

At a pivotal point in my life, it was a past life regression that opened up to me a whole new field of awareness and set me on a path of intense spiritual training. Shortly before I turned thirty I ended a relationship with a man whose spiritual beliefs were very different from my own. The relationship we shared was intense and volatile and it is clear to me now that I learned many things from this partnership but that they were not obvious to me at the time. Emotionally bruised and battered, I sought out appointments with psychics, healers and, in one case, a past life regression therapist. Free at last to pursue my interest in all things esoteric without fear of derision, I jumped in with both feet. I had begun to seek my truth.

My whole life I have had an inexplicable phobia of eyes. This has meant that visiting the optometrist has proved to be a very traumatic experience over the years and in fact on one occasion I actually bit one poor man on the hand! I have burst into tears on public transport, run screaming from a cinema and gone to extraordinary lengths to avoid confronting my fear and so I wondered whether undergoing a past life regression might shed any light on why on earth I could cheerfully visit the dentist or doctor, happily put my head under water or travel by plane, but could not hear anyone telling me about their laser eye surgery without having a panic attack. That I chose to do this following the end of an emotionally abusive relationship only underlines for me the fact that I was seeking more than an interesting experience or the root of a phobia. I was making an attempt to eliminate fear from my life.

This event took place almost twenty years ago but the details of it are still searingly bright to me. The first thing I remember is telling the practitioner, a woman named Sue, that I was just qualifying as a reflexologist. She looked at me knowingly and said, "Ah yes, that's how I started out on this path too." I wondered what she meant. She asked why I was there and I told her about my eye phobia and my keenness to explore it and possibly even diminish its power. She began a kind of light hypnosis and while she did so, I "saw" a series of images playing out on the space behind my forehead, which always looks like a cinema screen to me. This is where I "see" any psychic images when I work with Spirit; where information is shown to me. Before I knew what I was doing, I was describing to her my life in what appeared to be a medieval settlement of some kind. Sue asked me to look down at my feet and to my surprise I saw that I was wearing sackcloth and that my feet were dirty and in very worn, scuffed wrap-over cloth shoes. I thought I was in a country that might now be known as Germany or France; this wasn't based on anything other than a kind of inner knowing. The place where I lived appeared to be a settlement with lots of huts grouped together and carts being pulled around. It was cold and sparse. I told Sue that I was a woman in my twenties living with a daughter aged around four and my father. I did not know where the father of my child was but I felt that perhaps he had left our village to fight or go to some kind of war and not returned. My mother was dead.

I spent a few moments observing myself in this former life before Sue asked me to tell her what I was doing. At first I appeared to be undertaking normal everyday tasks for that time such as carrying pails of water around, tending to chickens and preparing food over a meagre fire, but then something interesting happened. I saw myself sitting inside my hut and a young man entered. I talked with him for a while and then started spreading out what looked like Tarot cards on the floor between us. What was interesting is that these were not Tarot cards as I recognised them. Bear in mind that my knowledge of Tarot was all fairly new to me at this point, and so in my mind, the imagery of the iconic Rider-Waite deck was what I would have expected to see. These cards, however, were unlike anything I had ever encountered before. They were much taller than the cards I knew and a sepia colour, all browns and yellows, rather than the bright colours we normally associate with the art. I exclaimed, "Oh, I'm a seer!" – not a term I would normally have used.

As I observed myself in my hut, I had a knowing that the man who had come to seek my advice was not somebody I was comfortable with. I felt that, in this story being played out, he wanted me to be with him but that my loyalties were still with the absent father of my child. I knew that practising any kind of psychic arts such as card reading or clairvoyance was somehow forbidden in this society and I began to get a very uneasy feeling as I saw the scene advance. Sure enough, the image then jumped to a group of men on horseback who were dressed like soldiers. I knew that the man in my hut had somehow betrayed me to them and they came to my hut and took me away. I can still remember the agony of being torn apart from my young daughter and that I called out to my father to look after her. I knew that I would not return.

Sue then asked me to fast forward to how I ended that particular life and I immediately saw myself in some kind of underground environment on the outskirts of my village. I saw my body lying face down on the dirt floor and knew that I had been terribly violated. She asked me to zoom in closer and as I began to do so I gained the horrifying realisation that because I had been uncovered as a seer, my torture had involved having my eyes put out. In these early cultures, you either subscribed to the belief that there were realms beyond our knowledge, respecting the information that came to us from them, or you were fearful. Those in control – kings, lords, people who governed – were of course fearful as they often ruled by fear themselves and kept the illiterate villagers down with threats and brutality. If a seer were to assure the people that their elite rulers were little more than bullies then their power would be gone, so they did everything they could to rid themselves of anyone who represented this type of threat.

What struck me most about this part of the regression was that it wasn't at all upsetting to see my past life self in this way. I felt detachment and curiosity as to what was happening to "me" as each stage unfolded. I realised that by the time I was viewing my lifeless body, my spirit had already left it and was hovering a few feet above, observing. As the session drew to a close, Sue asked me whether I had any feeling as to what my name might be and I was surprised to hear my voice blurt out the word, "Althea," with very precise pronunciation: "Al-tay-ah"; a name that I'm pretty sure I was not aware of previously.

Ever since that regression my eye phobia has been a lot less intense. In addition, many years before I had children I had commented to friends that I didn't know why but I thought I would only ever have sons. For some reason I didn't think that I would be a very good mother to daughters. After the regression I stopped having this feeling and began to imagine that a girl or girls might be a part of my future after all. Whether my uncertainty was down to some kind of premonition that one of my daughters would not live long in this life, or to a harking back to this past life memory, I do not yet know.

I am certain that my daughter in that lifetime was my older daughter Layla in this lifetime. At the end of the regression I looked to see what happened to my young daughter and I saw that she became an exceptionally independent woman and travelled far, which must have been a rarity in those times. Layla is a strong, free-spirited girl with a very real fear of being separated from me at times. She often expresses a desire to look after me and make sure I'm okay, which I find odd coming from a seven-year-old girl. She's without doubt an old soul with very strong psychic abilities and I just know that we have been together many times before.

I am also certain that Layla visited me in some way before she was born. The notion of "conscious conception" is an area that was of great interest to me during my time as a reflexologist working with fertility, and the thought-provoking book *Spirit Babies* by Walter Makichen is a title that I would recommend to many of my clients. Walter Makichen was a medium who worked with those wishing to conceive a child or those who had experienced the trauma of a termination, miscarriage or child loss. He had a theory that we are all assigned a number of possible children during this lifetime and claimed to be able to see these children in the aura of a woman or couple. What's more, he held that we are able to communicate with our child or children to come and that whether or not they choose to join us in this incarnation is a matter of choice between the soul of the incoming child and the parents he or she has selected.

Early in 2007 Darius and I began to talk about the possibility of starting a family. I knew from my work with fertility how pressurised this decision can be so we made a pact to be as relaxed as possible about it and to trust that the children who were meant to be with us would come at the right time. To be honest, my reflexology practice at that time was so busy I hardly gave the business of my own possible pregnancy a second thought until one day at the end of a yoga class.

I was lying on my back on the floor, relaxing in the final pose of yoga, Shivasana. I attended this particular class regularly, always making time for it in between criss-crossing back and forth across London to give home visits to my reflexology clients. Practising yoga really helped me to stretch out my body and relax my mind and I was committed to making this time for myself. The class was a popular one in the middle of London's trendy Notting Hill and on this particular day I was positioned towards the back of a crowded studio. Lying still and focusing on my breath, I suddenly and very distinctly heard the voice of a child say, "Mummy." This was so unexpected that I immediately sat bolt upright to look. The yoga centre did not run children's classes, apart from a baby massage class at the weekend and there was a crèche downstairs for babies and toddlers. I wondered with mild alarm whether a child could possibly have wandered up from downstairs and be looking for their mother. My mat was right next to the door, which I had not heard open, and sure enough when I looked there was no child. I lay back down again. Then, on my "cinema screen" I saw very clearly a little girl aged about four years old. She looked identical to me but had Darius's curly hair and she looked straight at me and said, "Mummy." Then she was gone.

When I got home, something told me to take a pregnancy test and I was surprised to find that I was, indeed, pregnant. I told Darius and added, "I know this sounds crazy but I'm sure I saw this baby today. She was around four years old, she looked just like me but with your hair and she called me Mummy." Sadly, a few days later I experienced heavy blood loss and the pregnancy was gone. As I was only around six or seven weeks pregnant at the time, this is what is sometimes known as a "chemical pregnancy". In the days before the sophisticated pregnancy tests that we have now it's unlikely that I would have known I was pregnant at all, and the bleed would probably have registered as heavier than normal menstruation. Of course, this information didn't help me at all at the time and I was terribly upset but accepted that it wasn't the right time for this baby yet.

Almost exactly a year to the day later I fell pregnant again. Naturally I spent the whole pregnancy absolutely convinced that I was expecting the girl I had seen in that yoga class. The arrival of a son was not at all what I had been expecting but I am not an easy person to surprise and this was a large part of the reason that we opted not to know the gender of any of our children during pregnancy. Kasper was one of the best surprises I ever had.

I did feel puzzled whenever I thought about that experience in the yoga class though. As the weeks and months passed, it stayed detailed and crystal clear in my mind; usually a good indication that what I have seen isn't down to my imagination. However, I told myself that I had clearly got this one completely wrong. When Kasper was ten months old we invited our next child to join us and just after nine months later Layla arrived in a whirlwind birth lasting just 45 minutes. As I gazed at her in the moments afterwards the thought slowly dawned that somehow these two children had agreed between them to rearrange the order in which they would be born into our family. I kept thinking, "She was supposed to be first, but they switched!" I tried to dismiss these thoughts, especially as I thought that I would never know the truth, but they persisted.

Once Layla reached the age at which she was starting to talk, she began to try and say, "Mama." If you have children you may know that words beginning with the letter "m" can present some challenges, which is why many children manage the word "Dada" or "Daddy" first. "Mummy" usually comes after they've attempted "Mama", which is a little easier for them to form. Always linguistically adept from a very early age, Kasper called me "Mama" from the outset and in fact still uses this name for me but right from the start, to my surprise, Layla would say "Mummy". I couldn't work out where she had heard the word, as Kasper was resolutely sticking to "Mama" and this is the name Darius would use to refer to me too. One day as I sat quietly feeding Layla I suddenly said, "I know why you keep saying Mummy. It was you that day at the yoga class wasn't it, and you're letting me know it was you by calling me by that name even though it's different from what your brother says." From that day onwards she began to say, "Mama," and I didn't hear her use "Mummy" again for some years.

As if this wasn't proof enough for me, not long afterwards I visited a psychic medium. She began by referring to my two children and told me confidently that I had an older girl and then a boy. Not wanting to give her too much information or "lead" her in any way, I answered that, yes, I did have two children. She asserted once again that the girl was the eldest. I answered that no, she wasn't. The medium looked momentarily confused and apologised, saying that she was usually very accurate with this type of information and that she was being shown very definitively that my daughter had come first. Before I had a chance to reply she said, "Oh, I see! Your daughter was supposed to come first but they swapped places, didn't they?" To me, this is an astonishing piece of accuracy that confirms exactly what I already knew for myself.

What I found even more astounding was that when Layla reached four years old – the year that Romy was born and the age that I knew my daughter was in the past life regression – she appeared exactly as the little girl I had seen in my yoga class had looked. She looks just like me, and until the age of five she had beautiful curly hair, just like Darius. The past life regression I experienced way back before I had even met my husband opened my mind up to all sorts of possibilities and I find it fascinating to consider the scenario that my children chose me. Layla has remarkable insight and often makes comments or tells me things that have led me to realise that she has strong psychic ability. I feel that she has chosen to be my daughter in this lifetime to continue the relationship from the previous lifetime I saw in my regression that was cut short when "I" died. We have much to learn from each other.

After the regression I did some research on the name Althea and discovered that it was an Old English name possibly derived from Greek, meaning "with healing power". This presented me with a big piece of the jigsaw. At that time I was working in PR for a large animal charity and hoped to practise reflexology as a sideline. For the first time, I began to wonder whether I could find a way to truly recognise my purpose and make healing my priority. I asked myself whether I could still be a healer and a seer in this current lifetime, continuing the work I had begun but which was cut short in that previous existence.

Prompt: Get a piece of paper ready and write down the first answer that comes into your head. Write impulsively and using your instinct; do not question whatever pops into your mind, and whatever you do, don't overthink it. It can be one word, a phrase, a person, place or belief. Keep it safe until you reach the end of this book. Here it comes:

What is your truth? Where do you find it?

Chapter 2

Starting to See

Vision is the art of seeing what is invisible to others.
– Jonathan Swift

To explain how I came back to my path, I need to explain how I got on it in the first place. As a child I was an advanced and prolific reader, devouring the works of the Brontë sisters, Dickens, Shakespeare and Thomas Hardy by the time I was thirteen. I loved school, and particularly English assignments where we were asked to complete a piece of creative writing. Closeted in my bedroom, I would spend hours writing and I can still remember the liberating and strangely out of control feeling of letting the words flow through me and on to the page. At the age of eleven I remember being asked to show a visiting dignitary to our school one of my stories. He read the whole thing in silence and then turned to my teacher and said, "It's extraordinary. She writes like Dickens!" I doubt I will ever score a better compliment than that.

By the time I was twelve or thirteen I was churning out stories, poems and plays on a typewriter my parents bought me. I would beg them to let me go to our local library every Friday after school where I would spend hours browsing the aisles. I would always come home with a selection of biographies of interesting people from history, literature or film, some classic I hadn't yet read and something from the paranormal section. I rounded off my weekly solo trip with a stop at the petrol station on the corner of my road to buy a chocolate bar. I entered writing competitions, earning myself a highly commended in one large national short story competition and once even wrote an entire play which I managed to persuade the headmaster to allow me to put on at school. I directed my whole class, organised some of my fellow students into costume design and special effects (I seem to remember that indoor fireworks and smoke bombs were involved – Health and Safety was somewhat non-existent during the 1980s) and acted in it myself. I thought my path in life was set.

Life, however, had different ideas.

I read avidly throughout my childhood, particularly encouraged by my dad, Ray, who had always instilled in me the knowledge that, as long as you could read well, you could do anything. An intelligent man with charm, humour and natural people skills, my father didn't have the best of opportunities as a child and consequently ended up in what used to be known as a Secondary Modern school; basically a school for those who weren't expected to amount to much academically. How wrong he proved them to be, by working hard, reading as much as he could and studying to successfully put himself through A levels. He enjoyed a long and interesting career with the Civil Service, retiring at the enviable age of 51; not bad for someone who wasn't given to believe he could be a high flyer. Dad always took an interest in our schoolwork and I remember in particular discussing my creative writing assignments with him. After our family dinner I would approach him with my essay topic in hand and we would discuss the subject matter and the structure of the piece before I finally took myself off upstairs to write it. From a young age I was always a night owl and my mother says she can still remember the sound of my typewriter clattering away into the small hours. My father also fuelled my interest in the paranormal. Every Christmas I could hardly wait to find the book in my stocking, always selected by him and always to do with ghosts, the paranormal or mediumship.

My mother Vivienne was and still is a constant source of calm support in all our lives and has had psychic abilities for as long as I can remember. Although she is very reluctant to recognise it, my mother is a creative person and watching her engaging with various domestic creative activities as a child influenced me greatly. Thanks to my mother, I grew up with the belief that I could make things. This may at first seem to relate only to the physical, but I also attribute to this the fact that throughout my life I have always believed that I can make things happen. We weren't perpetually ferried about from one extracurricular activity to another, in part because there wasn't enough money but also because my parents enjoyed being with us.

I grew up with my younger sister, Claire, and like many other families in Britain in the 1970s our life was relatively simple. Unlike today, there wasn't a huge choice of extracurricular activities and classes to distract us and the spare time we had outside school allowed us to play long, imaginative games, combatting boredom and offsetting squabbles by using our imaginations. We were allowed to watch television but the choice of children's programmes was limited and so we spent a lot of time reading and playing together instead. Of course, there were arguments but we were encouraged to find a way of working through them. My sister's personality is more reserved and down to earth than mine and over the years she has been the perfect foil to my more dramatic, "over the top" nature. Hers was always the voice of reason and throughout our childhood there were many occasions on which I wished I had listened to her before leaping into my latest scheme. Our polar opposite characters have stood us in good stead and despite our fundamental differences we have always been very close. Hers is an opinion I would always trust without question and I often wonder whether we chose this lifetime as sisters as a lesson in achieving perfect balance.

I find it refreshing to recall that there was very little expectation on our part as children growing up; like our parents before us, to a certain extent we had to seek our own entertainment. As very small children we were simply carried along on whatever activity my mother happened to need to do that day: grocery shopping, a trip to the market, visiting the local haberdashery store to choose fabrics for her to make us dresses. On rainy days she would make us a den using a blanket draped over the dining room chairs and we'd spend ages in there playing while she hummed away on her sewing machine. Our holidays were usually taken somewhere in the UK up until the year I was seven, when my mum worked on a factory production line making sweets for several weeks in order to save enough money to take us on our first family holiday abroad, to Mallorca. My dad was always home from work in time to sit down and have dinner with us; even turning down a work promotion as it would mean he wouldn't get home in time to be with us in the evenings. We even sat down to breakfast together most days.

Everything was discussed as a family; something that I have tried to replicate with my own children. Nothing was hidden from us and big questions were always discussed, which meant that we were stronger as a unit whenever some issue or problem occurred. We would talk a lot about spirituality when we were growing up and my mum always explained with great honesty how she never used to believe in life after death, ghosts, spirits or the paranormal in any way at all. My paternal grandfather, Stuart, was always interested in spirituality and would often end up in a discussion about the afterlife with his daughter-in-law, my mother, during which she would be adamant that she didn't believe in anything of the sort. "You wait," he would tell her. "When I'm gone I'm going to come back and show you that I'm right!"

And so he did.

I have vivid recollections of this grandfather, even though he passed to Spirit when I was just shy of four years old. He was diagnosed with cancer at the end of October 1977 and by 1st December of the same year (oddly, the date on which I am sitting here writing this chapter today) he had passed. I have been told that, even before knowing he was ill, I would arrive at my grandparents' house, pull up a footstool and sit next to his wing chair, wordlessly holding his hand for hours. I remember arriving the morning after he had passed and keenly feeling the shift in energy in the house. "He's gone to be with the angels," my grandmother told me, and this seemed an acceptable truth to me. Over the years I held many "conversations" with this grandfather, often at night just before I went to sleep. These conversations were in a sense one-sided as I would just chat away to him. To me, there were clear responses as I would ask my granddad what to do in certain situations and always felt as if I received some kind of guidance. I have felt my grandfather's presence with me my whole life, to the point that although he passed when I was so young I always felt that I knew him personally much better than I could have done in reality. Over the years, whenever I have visited mediums for a sitting my grandfather Stuart has very often come through. He and my own father were very much alike, and I have frequently been asked by mediums whether my father is in spirit as they have believed him, rather than my grandfather, to have shown up. On one such occasion, Dad was in fact sitting on a chair just behind me. Much hilarity ensued when the medium asked, "Tell me, dear, is your father in spirit?" to which I replied quick as a flash, "I hope not – the last time I looked he was sitting over there!" She went on to describe my grandfather to me; whom of course I had known all along was with us because I could feel his presence too. I have come to recognise him, not just as my grandfather but as a sort of extra spirit guide.

It was this grandfather who provided me with my first solid experience of seeing Spirit at the age of fourteen. My parents began planning a move from Maidstone – the small riverside town in the southeast that I'd grown up in – to Luton, a larger town further towards the middle of the country. I was settled in an all-girls grammar school with my two best friends Michelle and Emma and did not under any circumstances want to leave. My dad – at that time, senior management with the Civil Service – had gone for a big promotion and he got the job. I could sense that my parents were happy and excited about the new opportunity, but also that they were terribly worried about the prospect of uprooting my sister and I from our childhood home and friends. So I tried my best to hide my sadness and anxiety.

Our big move was to happen in two stages. Dad's job started before we managed to find a new house and relocate, so for a time he commuted up and down the M1 motorway at either end of the week and stayed in a hotel. He returned home at weekends and sometimes nipped back on a Wednesday night too – leaving very early on Thursday morning for the drive back up the motorway – because he missed us so much. One weekend, we were all talking around the table when Dad started to tell us about what had happened during his Wednesday drive home that past week. He had been driving behind a long open truck carrying metal scaffolding poles all lashed together when the traffic had slowed suddenly and without warning. Dad said that as he'd looked up he saw all the metal poles in front of him hurtling towards the car windscreen, ends first. He slammed on his brakes but the situation was so terrifying he actually put his hands up in a vain attempt to protect his head. He knew, he said, that this was serious injury or death.

Then a very strange thing happened. He heard an almighty crunch, and when he looked up, the poles had hit the front headlight of his car, missing the windscreen entirely. The angle had the poles heading straight for the windscreen at speed and there wasn't room enough for them to divert their course. Just as Dad was finishing his story I heard a voice in my head saying, "It was your grandfather. He pushed the poles." At the same time I had an image of my granddad in my mind's eye – that space at the front of my mind, behind where my forehead is. I have come to learn that when I "see" things clairvoyantly, they very often appear or play out on this space like a movie. Without thinking, I blurted out, "They're saying it was Granddad who moved the poles. They would never have done that by themselves, there wasn't time or space!" To give credit where it's due, neither of my parents batted an eyelid, or told me not to be so silly. They simply stopped their conversation, thought for a moment and accepted my comment with very little reaction.

A night or so later, I had another experience involving my granddad. With such incidences I have come to recognise that if I can remember the whole event in precise detail even many years later then it counts as a *bona fide* spiritual happening. It's always my litmus test when I begin to doubt myself or assume that I've finally lost it. This happened thirty years ago and I can still remember every detail as if it were yesterday.

It was a few weeks before our family was due to move and the reality of the situation had finally hit me. I had gone to bed that night feeling anxious and unsure of what the future might hold. I was fourteen years old and my position in my school life and social circle felt secure. I enjoyed performing in school plays, loved playing in the sports teams, especially netball, and had a small circle of very close friends. Two in particular, Michelle and Emma, I had known since I first started school and we were very close; always in and out of each other's houses when we weren't together in school. The thought of being without them every day was really hard, though I needn't have worried as over thirty years later we are all still in each other's lives and as close as we ever were.

I awoke at what felt like around 4 or 5am – I didn't check the time. It was summer, so the hours just before dawn broke still afforded a grey, gritty light and my curtains weren't too heavy so it was possible to see in the room. At the foot of my bed I saw a grey, shadowy figure which for a second alarmed me but when I looked more closely I realised I recognised it – it was my grandfather. I wasn't afraid; it simply felt as if a close family member, like my dad, had popped into the room to check on me and kiss me goodnight. It was a secure, friendly feeling of family – not at all like a visiting spectre.

I could see that Granddad was wearing old faded, baggy chinos (this proved to be significant later) and a dark green cable-knit fisherman's sweater. I did not recall particularly remembering him in these clothes; he had, you remember, passed ten years previously when I had been only four. His face seemed blurry but the rest of him was as clear as it could be in the predawn light. I remember sitting bolt upright in bed in amazement, saying, "I can't believe it! You've actually come back to see me after all this time!" I had been talking to this grandfather in Spirit and sensing him around me for years, but actually seeing him at the foot of my bed was a whole new experience for me, and I was struggling to accept what I was seeing. At this point he moved towards me and as he did so he went out of focus and I started to see the room spinning a little. Inexplicably, as I looked at the walls I could see all the wallpaper peeling away to the extent that I could tell you which paper and design was underneath for at least six layers back. Then I looked again and he was kneeling next to my bed, just as if he were kissing me goodnight or telling me a bedtime story.

It was then that I became aware of a woman. I couldn't see her; it was as if she were standing just outside my vision, behind my right shoulder. She was talking into my right ear, as if acting as a sort of interpreter for my granddad, who didn't speak. I was slightly taken aback to hear that she had a broad Lancashire accent. At fourteen, I didn't really know what a Lancashire accent sounded like but I just knew that this woman spoke with one. Also, although I couldn't physically see her, I knew that she was in her mid to late fifties with curly dark hair. In my spiritual work since, I've come to associate anything I see, hear or feel spiritually on my right-hand side with the male side, and anything on the left with the female side. Since this was my paternal grandfather, this would fit. The woman spoke to me in a friendly, chatty way, like a neighbour you know well. "He's been very worried about you, you know," she said kindly. "And he's come to tell you that everything will be fine. You'll do really well in your new life. And he says it was him who helped your father."

And then, they were both gone. I must have fallen back to sleep, and when I woke up, it took me an hour or two to process what I thought had happened. Had it been a dream? Unusually, I felt reticent about telling my parents this because I didn't want to admit how worried I had been about the move. Eventually, I called Michelle, who was very down to earth and at the time pretty sceptical about such things, and told her what had happened. In particular, I remember telling her, "What he was wearing seems really significant. If I tell my mum and dad that then maybe it's some kind of proof." To my surprise, Michelle insisted that I told my mum. Over a cup of tea, I relayed my strange visitation to her and she countered it with a story of her own.

A few weeks after my grandfather's death, my mum had just put me to bed and as she came out on to the landing she saw standing there her father-in-law, as clear as day. He walked into my parents' bedroom and she followed him. As it was dusk, she switched on the light to see better and he disappeared. She took this as the proof he was always threatening to send her after he passed; proof of life after death. Ever since then she has believed firmly in The Other Side. Significantly, she told us, he was wearing a pair of old chinos and a bottle-green cable-knit sweater – his old favourite clothes which my nanna was always moaning about due to their scruffiness, but which he stubbornly continued to wear. Michelle and I almost fell off our chairs at this revelation – and we all knew that the spirit of my grandfather had paid me a visit. He seemed to have come to reassure me that I had nothing to worry about: my new life in Luton was going to be fine.

He was right too; it was more than fine. Claire and I settled into our new school, made good friends and I joined in with sports and various other extracurricular activities. It was at this school that I was allowed to put on the production of the play I wrote (something I doubt I would have been able to do at my previous school) and the headmaster turned out to be something of a mentor to me. He spotted an ability I didn't realise I had and entered me into an inter-county public speaking competition which our team (headed by me) won two years running. I was made Head Girl – a kind of school figurehead position – after just two terms. Even more amazing to me was the fact that *I knew* that these things were going to happen. On my first day in school the deputy headteacher took me on a walking tour and we stopped in front of an embossed wooden board in the main hall. On this board were the names of all the head boys and head girls from the school's history. I heard a voice tell me, "Your name is going to be on that board." At the time, that seemed ridiculous. I was crippled with nerves, missed my friends dreadfully and it took weeks for me to settle in properly. I enjoyed studying and spoke differently from other pupils at the school and so they poked fun at me for being "posh". It was clear to me right from the outset that I could either dumb myself down to fit in or I could believe that voice and gain some respect for pushing ahead. I'm happy to say that my strategy worked and I enjoyed my time at that school.

I am eternally grateful to my parents for always listening to and accepting my accounts of my spiritual experiences without judgement. This is something I hope that I am replicating with my own children, especially Layla, who has astounded me on more than one occasion with her references to experiences that, to my mind, are clearly spiritual ones. Talking to my children about what they sense and see has always held immense fascination for me and Layla caused me to consider this in a major way one night as I was putting her to bed. I have often found that she comes out with her musings just as she is drifting off to sleep. One evening, we had read a story and had just begun our nightly ritual of "I love yous". Half asleep, Layla murmured, "Mummy, I love you so much you won't believe it. I love you more than my other mummy." I pricked up my ears and tried to stop myself from blurting out a barrage of questions, wanting to take advantage of her sleepy state to extract as much information as possible.

"What other mummy, Layla? I'd love to hear about her." She looked at me askance, aware that she had said something that had piqued my interest; obviously asking herself whether admitting to having another mummy might provoke any feelings of envy in me, or worse, hurt my feelings. I kept my face neutral and encouraging and waited for a response.

"When I was in your tummy, silly. I had another mummy there with me, she sent me here and she would talk to me."

"That sounds lovely. What was she like? Can you tell me about her?"

"Well, she was older and sort of like a witch. She had special powers."

"Wow, how amazing. What else did she tell you?"

"I don't want to talk about her any more, Mummy, I want to go to sleep. I love you." And that was as much as she was willing to tell me.

We have co-slept with all our children and they know that they are still welcome in our bed whenever they feel the need. With Layla, there have always been far more incidents when she felt she needed to be with us at night and in fact ever since she was a very small child she has been reluctant to sleep alone. We've gone through various rigmaroles involving an arsenal of lighting equipment all designed to alleviate her fears: fairy lights, night lights, lamps on the landing, torches. Still, on some nights she would burst into our room very clearly afraid and upset, crawling into our bed and not wanting to go back to her own. One day I decided to tackle the issue with her and ask some questions to see whether there might be an underlying reason why she was so restless at night. As always, her answer astounded me.

"Layla," I asked, "is there a reason why you're waking up in the night do you think?" She looked at me as if I had just asked her whether she was a human being or a fish. "Well yes, Mummy," she said, slowly and carefully, as if the answer she was about to give me were blindingly obvious. "People talk to me at night when I'm trying to sleep and they wake me up."

"What people? What are they saying?"

"They want me to tell things to people. There are lots of them and they all want me to listen to them and tell people what they say." I felt a momentary chill while I pondered whether these voices, these people, could in any way be a malignant presence. My instinct told me that my daughter was simply experiencing what I have always known in my life: the presence of people in Spirit making a connection and wishing to pass messages to their families and loved ones here on earth. It was entirely possible that the voices Layla was hearing were members of our own family attempting to make contact with her or pass on guidance or advice. It was also possible that she was somehow communing with her spirit guides who felt that she was able to communicate their messages. Either way, my parental instinct kicked in and I resolved to help Layla gain distance from this presence that she clearly did not welcome.

"Okay," I asserted, "here's what we'll do. The next time any of these people wake you up or stop you from going to sleep, please explain to them kindly but very firmly that you need to go to sleep and tell them that whatever it is that they would like to say, they can say to Mummy." I went on to explain that I thought that these were spirit people who were talking to her, that she mustn't be afraid and that it was very special that they wanted to talk to her and that she could hear them, but that she must ask them to stop if she didn't want to listen. "Mummy," she asked, "can everyone hear spirit people like that? How does anyone get to sleep?"

"Well, no, actually not everyone can, but in our family I can hear them just like you can and so can Nanna. I don't mind talking to them or listening to them at all but you're only six and you need to get some sleep so they'll quite understand if you tell them that now's not a very good time to talk. They can say whatever they need to say to me."

"Okay, Mummy."

If I'm honest I didn't really think this would have any measurable effect. However, after that night Layla slept more soundly than she has done in years and her nocturnal visits to our bed have all but ceased. As always, I look for the obvious explanations. Was she making it all up? Has she simply grown out of it? Is it a fabrication designed to gain attention? I can't prove that it isn't, except to say that this has been an issue since she was very small and that I had never really talked to her about my spiritual beliefs or abilities before this conversation.

By far the most convincing display of Layla's abilities, however, came in the form of an innocent remark she made just a week or two before Romy died. It was late June and during bath time one evening I was chatting to the children about our plans for the approaching summer holidays. It's a tradition in our family to draw up a list of all the visits, activities and days out we would like to accomplish during the long summer break, based on the understanding that we all collectively agree on one activity per week. Of course, we never complete all the suggestions on the list but it's a lot of fun compiling it and has the added bonus of making things easier for Kasper, who is a great lover of routine and predictability.

This particular summer, a top activity for the list was a visit to a local outdoor swimming pool. We had visited the previous summer while I was pregnant with Romy and both children were keen to go back. I explained that we could, but that we would have to ask my friend Clare, an excellent swimmer who also happens to be fantastic with children, to accompany us as both of them were under eight years old, we would have Romy with us and it was too much for me to manage on my own. In the middle of our discussion Layla turned to me and asked, "Mummy, when Romy goes back, then will you be able to take me and Kasper to the outdoor pool on our own?"

"Sorry, what do you mean?"

"When Romy goes back. Will we be able to go swimming then on our own, just with you?"

My first thought was that this was a touch of wishful thinking mingled with sibling envy. Layla is a warm and loving child but occasionally aloof when she is unsure of a person or situation. She had been a little detached from Romy and I put this down to the fact that her sister's arrival had meant that not only was she no longer the only girl but also no longer the baby of the family. We were riding with it, giving her space to work it out. As she uttered this last sentence her expression changed and she looked as if she realised that she had said something she wasn't supposed to. I jumped in to counter it before she shut down completely.

"I'm not understanding properly, Layla. Can you find another way to tell Mummy what you mean?"

Layla looked me straight in the eye and said sincerely, "She's going back, Mummy." I admit that at this point my blood ran cold for a second and I registered the thought, "My God, what does she know that I don't?" but I quickly batted it away and inserted the sibling rivalry explanation again, embellishing this further with the idea that she also didn't fully understand that once you have a baby, the process cannot be reversed. After all, she was only four.

"When Romy goes back? Where is it that you think she's

going to go, darling?"

She began to look shifty. She had realised that I was all over this and decided to backpedal. Her next answer was more of a hesitant question: "Back in your tummy?" Relief flooded my whole being. Okay, she was just confused about where babies come from. I cobbled together a response that explained that once a baby is born, it stays in the family, just like she and Kasper had once been babies and then grown bigger. Did she understand? I will never forget the look on her face as she nodded yes. It was a placatory move. She knew that she had said something that wasn't run-of-the-mill and had made the conscious decision to quit trying to explain it and just go along with whatever made me feel happy. I felt uneasy as I helped the children out of the bath and the unease stayed with me until they were all asleep that night.

Call it grief, foolishness, naivety or whatever you will but I am convinced that Layla knew, on some deep level, that her sister would not be with us for long. As a small child, her transparency levels were so much greater than those of us who have learned to speak with caution and she simply spoke her truth.

Prompt: What can you remember from your own childhood that tells you that Spirit was near? Did you have an imaginary friend? Did you "know" things but were told not to be silly? If you have your own children, do they share insights with you involving unseen people or information they could not previously have known? Do they ever tell you about who they were before they came here?

Chapter 3

Shutting Down

There are cracks in everything. That's how the light gets in.
– Leonard Cohen

During my early twenties I "shut down". As my instinct to explore the physical world became stronger, I began to switch off my connection to Spirit as there was just too much going on. My focus turned towards all things material and physical, and I chose a series of relationships that were not only unsuccessful, but also unusual in their intensity and apparent unsuitability. I experienced others' addictions (to alcohol and drugs), mental and emotional abuse and one relationship that, at that point in my life, served only to highlight my own lack of integrity and self-respect. For almost a decade, I chose a path of destructive habits, insecurity, loneliness and confusion. During these years I lived in denial of my abilities and my path, but I believe that these negative experiences played a crucial role in setting the scene for what was to come. I have a strong belief that the individuals with whom these relationships played out were supporting me in my learning. You cannot experience light without dark, and you cannot teach or help others if you have never experienced difficulty.

When I look at my life now, I see the first part – childhood, school, university, first love, traumatic break-up, a huge variety of jobs – as a fairly inaccurate representation of who I really am. I was restless and unsettled; flitting from one job to another, always craving new experiences and struggling with being hypersensitive and feeling misunderstood. I lived with a persistent sense that there was something I was supposed to be doing accompanied by a constant nagging feeling that whatever

I was doing, this was not it. I was flighty and ungrounded. Then came my thirtieth birthday, which heralded a lot of change.

In the months leading up to it, I had been enjoying living in a London houseshare with two fantastic girls, Jacqui and Ciara. Ciara later moved out and we were joined by Leslie. All of us were single and had our own busy lives, but we formed such a bond living together that we are all still in touch over a decade later. Leslie hails from America and whenever one of us has occasion to cross the Atlantic we always go out of our way to visit the other. During this time, and after a couple of failed long-term relationships, I had chalked up four years of being single. My first serious relationship had resulted in an impetuous engagement at the age of 21 and ended with my then fiancé suddenly pulling the plug on the wedding within six months of the big day. I dallied with a highly unsuitable man for a few months after that and when I really hit rock bottom and saw that this relationship was going nowhere, I took drastic action. While visiting my friend Charlotte for the weekend I picked up a copy of a magazine she had lying around and idly began flicking through it and noticed that her flatmate had circled something in it. It was an advertisement looking for foreign language speakers to train and work as European tour guides, taking coach tours across several countries. Something in me clicked. "You should apply for that," Charlotte told me. "You speak languages and you're great with people." (At that time I spoke French and German well, having studied them at A-level.) Her flatmate passed by on the way to the kitchen and retorted, "There's no way you'll ever get an interview. I tried and I didn't even hear back from them." This was like a red rag to a bull and I put in an application the next week.

Little more than a month or two later I was a fully-fledged tour guide for Globus Cosmos, leading coach tours around Europe. I was happy to put my knowledge of languages to good use and within three months I also spoke fluent Italian. I did that job for almost four years until I got together with another tour guide and we quit the job to set up home together in London. This relationship, although it lasted for four years, was pretty intense and, as it turned out, unhealthy. My boyfriend enjoyed a drink and it wasn't long before I began to see that this was causing him to behave in some unbalanced and sometimes unpleasant ways. He didn't have any time whatsoever for anything of an esoteric nature and neither did he appreciate my interest in it. There were many violent, alcohol-fuelled arguments and I eventually made the decision to leave. It's now obvious to me that this is a phase during which my psychic abilities were very much "switched off"; either due to the fact that I was too busy drinking, partying and playing at being married or because I picked partners who weren't particularly spiritually open. My instincts were dulled; I couldn't make a decision to help my own life and happiness, let alone advise anyone else. I chose two relationships that seemed to provide me with very emotionally intense experiences, not much of which felt very positive at the time.

Looking back, I now understand the reason why I chose this path (and believe me, I did choose it). I consider it a kind of training. The relationship that almost saw me married at 23 was a happy one up until the point that my boyfriend decided to dabble in drugs. Of course, this relationship was never going to survive as we were so young and such different choices were being made but what it taught me was that I have a strong mind, that I am not swayed by what others think or do and that I never give up in times of extreme difficulty. I obviously hadn't learned the key lesson I had chosen for myself though as what did I do next? Pick a relationship with a man who had a heavy dependency on alcohol. It took me two relationships over a combined total of seven years to learn that you cannot "cure" someone else's addiction with the power of your love. I learned that addiction is a powerful master and can only be conquered by its subject. I also learned never, ever to judge anyone with any type of dependency. Finally, I learned that the relationship you choose very often reflects the view you have of yourself; so if you have chosen as your life partner an individual whose sense of self-worth is so low that they have a dependency on an addictive substance, what does that say about you? We pick the relationship we think we deserve and also that which often reflects what we ourselves have to learn. These partnerships caused me to look closely at my own addictive personality and how this plays out, for better or worse, in my own life. It took me a very long time to emerge from "victim mode" ("Why do I always end up with these men? Why have I been treated so poorly?") and to begin to feel compassion and understanding for the choices that these individuals made and my reasons for choosing to share a portion of my life with them.

During my four years working as a tour guide in Europe my spiritual self didn't fare much better than my physical body, which I was abusing with alcohol and cigarettes. I was still hurting from my perceived rejection from my previous relationship and searching for whomever or whatever it was I felt would "complete" me. I took pride in my work, enjoying learning about countries I had previously never visited and imparting that learning to people on my tours, but in private I was lonely, angry and full of self-doubt. I really didn't like myself very much at all. Added to this, I soon discovered that while there were many positive aspects to life as a tour guide, the enjoyment of the job really depended on who you had on your coach. On most tours the group would be full of wonderful, appreciative people but there would always be one or two negative-minded individuals who seemed determined to see the fault in everything. This job taught me a lot about human nature and how to deal with challenges. During it, I found myself standing on a pavement in Paris with a short American man inches from my face, screaming at me at the top of his voice because his room did not have air conditioning. On a ferry crossing from Bari to Patras I was awoken in the middle of the night by a sweaty Greek lorry driver repeatedly trying the handle of the door to my room, and I had to lock myself in my bedroom in Rome after a waiter I had asked for help in getting an out-of-hours emergency snack for a diabetic passenger decided to take me on a late night tour of the kitchen. My poor parents received numerous distress calls from me, detailing the latest drama or problem. As a parent myself now I dread to think how many sleepless nights that job of mine must have given them.

After I made the decision to stop gallivanting around Europe on a coach I remarked that there would never be another job that presented me with as many challenges as that one had, and I was pretty much right. After dealing with the extreme end of these human emotions I honestly felt that I could take on anything the world of work threw at me. I also ended up with enough stories to fill another book. It was just as well that I emerged feeling so capable as over the next few years I continued to lurch from one career path to another, never finding the happiness or satisfaction that I was seeking. I do not recall in all this time having any psychic experiences. My instinct, or gut feeling, usually so reliable, seems to have totally switched off and left me. "Why shouldn't it?" I thought bitterly to myself on the odd occasion I tried to fire it up. "No one else wants to be with me either."

Once I returned to London I found myself a job in a busy architect's firm as PA to the managing director. One day, a regular client was passing through the reception area and happened to make a remark to me in French. Much to his surprise, I replied in French and this was the beginning of a long personal friendship that endures to this day. At that time, Bill was setting up his own executive search business and asked me if I would like to come and work with him. Part of that job involved dealing with a large, US non-profit organisation advising on land use and within a year I found myself hopping on and off planes, travelling to European capital cities to organise events and coordinate individual country councils. Twice a year, I travelled to the States to attend large-scale conferences. Life was hectic, exciting and full of exclusive restaurants, fancy hotels and eye-opening city tours to marvel at various architectural delights. Sometimes, my previous skills as a tour guide were called upon as I was asked to provide personalised city tours of some of my old haunts to visiting American dignitaries. Bill was a great mentor to me and joked that he was my "stand-in dad" during the trips we took as he always had my back. I got to know his wife and their children well, and always appreciated his generosity as an employer. He taught me a lot about always helping those further down the ladder than yourself; finding their areas of expertise and helping them to shine. Bill is also a talented photographer and one of my most treasured possessions is a photograph he took of me with Romy, just a week before she passed. I am so glad that he had the chance to meet her.

I look back at this time of my life with great fondness and see now that the very grounded nature of this work – helping to provide a platform for others to discuss best ethical use of land and planning cityscapes – was a perfect balance to my more ethereal spiritual tendencies. I feel that, by putting me in a position of roundedness and connecting me with networks of people all over the world, this role was in some way preparing me for my future work. It was during this period, at the end of January 2000 after a trip to Rio de Janeiro to see in the new millennium, that I finally made the decision to leave my volatile relationship. I continued to travel and then, in November 2000, another seminal event occurred. My beloved grandmother passed to Spirit.

Sylvia May Rees was born in the Welsh Valleys on 29th March 1913. Almost exactly sixty years later, on 30th March 1973, I arrived and forty-one years after that, on 26th March 2014, Romy made her entrance to this world. For this reason, we chose to give

Romy the middle name Silvia. My grandmother Sylvia was a feisty, energetic and opinionated woman who also had a natural talent for healing. She left her tiny Welsh village at the age of 14 and travelled to Colwyn Bay to train as a nurse. She chose her vocation well and carried on through the war years, during which she drove ambulances (even though she repeatedly failed her driving test in post-war years). She and my grandfather Stuart had their share of difficulties but loved each other deeply and it was she who nursed him with devotion during the last months of his illness with cancer. I remember my grandmother for her feistiness, her guttural laugh and exclamations of random Welsh words. She was always creating something or trying out a new diversion, some of those I remember being knitting tea cosies, crochet, winemaking, some downright outlandish culinary experiments and nail and thread artwork. I would sit for hours with her after Sunday lunch at our house, learning to crochet and listening to her tall stories.

My grandmother had been becoming increasingly frail for some years prior to her passing. Not so that you'd particularly notice, but she'd lost some of her verve. At eighty-seven, she was finally slowing down. She spent several weeks in hospital and my parents drove up and down the motorway to sit with her and help to keep her house running while she was incapacitated. At some point, she took a turn for the worse and we started gathering close as a family, supporting each other and trying to provide a constant presence for her. My sister Claire, herself a nurse and at that time a new mother to our eldest nephew, took it upon herself to visit one day after my father told her that Nanna was failing. Typically, during this visit my grandmother sprang to life, bossing Claire around and appearing for all the world like a woman full of energy and chomping at the bit to get out of hospital. My sister has since nursed many people as their time approaches and has spoken about how they often "rally" and appear to be full of boundless energy in their final days.

The following week, I took some days off work to relieve my parents, who desperately needed some time at home after weeks of shuttling back and forth to the hospital. On the day I arrived, I took my seat by my grandmother's bedside, held her hand and listened as she appeared to be speaking to people I could not see. After a while she registered my presence, spoke to me by name and told me how glad she was to see me. I will never forget that she said to me, "I know we all have to go. But why does it have to take so long?" Hers was not a comfortable passing. For whatever reason, she needed to experience a gradual letting go. Instinctively, I leaned closer, held her hand tightly and said, "It's your choice, Nanna. It's okay for you to let go whenever you need to go. We all love you very much. There's nothing left to hang on for." I knew that she was holding on to her position as the family matriarch; reluctant to let go and leave her sons, whom she loved fiercely. As soon as I spoke these words to her, she went into cardiac arrest right in front of me. I leapt back, terrified, afraid that my words had somehow caused this to happen (which I now see that in a way they did). I ran to find a doctor and, had I not been present, I feel sure that the medical professionals would have let her slip away. Instead, they worked to the best of their ability to show that they were doing all they could to save her. This puzzled me, because I knew that my grandmother knew that she was at the end of her life. She was beginning to accept this, and to facilitate her own passing. However, our human instinct is to try to prolong life, no matter what.

She was rushed into theatre and they took measures to strengthen her heart artificially to keep her alive. I held her hand as they wheeled her in, semi-conscious on a gurney, and she turned to me, looked me directly in the eyes and said, "I'll be coming back to you." I knew that she was not stating her intention to return from theatre. She was telling me that she would return to me from the afterlife. We had had many conversations about this and I had always told her, half-jokingly, "You'd better come back and see me after you've gone!" As it turned out, she did return from theatre but never fully regained consciousness. My parents arrived, and we sat by her bedside together as she drifted in and out of consciousness. She continued to speak to people who appeared to be just beyond where we were sitting; muttering incoherently to them and occasionally smiling. At the end of visiting hours my parents left for the night and we agreed that they would return home to rest. I was the designated point of contact for the hospital as I was staying with Michelle, who lived close by. That night, I had a fitful sleep dreaming of my grandmother and my grandfather. Somewhere around 2am, the phone rang. It was the hospital. I hung up and dialled my parents' number straight away to tell my father that his mother had passed.

From very early on, I felt my grandmother's presence around me. I was living alone at the time in a basement flat in south London, working as PR Manager for Battersea Dogs & Cats Home and I often fostered dogs from the shelter. One night, a dog I was looking after became very excitable just outside my bedroom door. I had had him for some nights and he had never exhibited this behaviour before. When I went out to him, he was whining and half barking at an empty space beside a small table on which I had photographs of various family members, including my grandmother. On another occasion, I got up in the night to visit the bathroom and as I walked past that table I had an overwhelming sense of my grandmother's unmistakably strong presence. Several months after that, during a trip to Rome with my parents we were sitting in a restaurant and reminiscing about her when my father suddenly exclaimed that he could smell her perfume. There were no other diners sitting near us at the time and neither my mother nor I were wearing perfume of any kind.

Three days after she had passed I was staying at my parents' home and was disturbed by a dream. In it, my grandmother was behind what looked like a pane of glass. She was gesticulating behind it as if she had to tell me something urgently, but I couldn't hear her. I found this upsetting and, eventually wide awake, I went downstairs to get a glass of water. I found my father in the kitchen and asked him what he was doing up at that early hour and he described to me exactly the same dream as I had just experienced. Extraordinarily, my grandmother somehow seemed to have been able to appear to both my father and myself in the same dream on the same night. Neither of us ever found out what it was she seemed be so keen to tell us, but knowing her as the lively, communicative person that she was in life, I suspect that we were simply witnessing her frustration at trying to communicate with us and not being heard.

I have come to sense her presence most when I am cooking; something we often enjoyed together. I always feel her presence just behind my right shoulder and find myself throwing a random ingredient into the mix or measuring something by eye – both her style rather than mine. In years to come this detail would be mentioned to me more than once by mediums I visited. I still sometimes feel her with me in the kitchen and the last time she came through to me, in a reading with the medium Claire Broad in 2017, I was told, "She says she cooks with you. She stands to your right and supervises things." She continues to be a major inspiration and influence in my life from the other side.

The week following her passing, I was sent on a work trip to Prague. It was early December, it was snowing and the city was truly magical but I felt empty, cold and alone. One morning, I woke and stumbled out of bed to look out of the window and an unsettling thing happened: I had no earthly idea where I was. I looked round the hotel room; it was the same nondescript decor found in many of the other hotels I stayed in regularly. I couldn't tell it from the last one I had visited. I looked out of the window again and tried to identify my location from the architecture and city layout. Was I in Germany? I turned on the TV, expecting to hear the familiar sound of German, a language I spoke well. To my horror, I didn't recognise a single word. I found the whole experience deeply disturbing and when I returned to London at the end of that job I marched into the office and told them that I was resigning because I no longer knew which city I was in when I woke up. They weren't impressed, but I paid attention to my instincts and took the leap of faith. As always, it paid off.

Knowing that I was about to finish a job with no other employment lined up, I decided to apply for a credit card. I wanted to choose one that benefitted a charity, so I picked Battersea Dogs & Cats Home and filled out their online application form. As I was about to hit "send", I heard a voice in my ear tell me, "Attach your CV." This sounded as ridiculous to me then as it looks on the page now, but I knew better than to dismiss it, so I did attach my CV. The very next day I received a call from a woman who introduced herself as Sarah Ruff from Battersea Dogs Home. Naturally, I thought this was a joke and almost hung up, but in actual fact, she was the PA to the Director General. She told me that he would like to meet with me and when I peered at him across his smoke-filled office a few days later (this was in the days before smoking bans), a remarkable exchange took place:

"I just had to invite you in because never before have I met anyone who sends their CV in with a charity credit card application. Are you mad?"

"No, I'm not mad but I've always wanted to work with an animal charity so I just thought I'd give it a try."

"Well, our PR Manager's just left. Do you want that job?"

"I'd love the job, but I don't have any PR experience, just marketing and events. I have a marketing qualification and I'm a good communicator. I can write well…"

"Yes, yes, never mind about that, you'll pick it up on the job. Speak to Sarah on your way out and she'll sort you out with a contract."

As the saying goes: truth is often stranger than fiction and this was the way I landed myself a job as Public Relations Manager for Battersea Dogs & Cats Home; a position I remained in for four years, which was a long time for me. I had a strong attachment to this job, a feeling I shared with many other staff members as we felt ourselves champions to the abandoned, mistreated and lonely dogs and cats that ended up in our care. We all felt a sense of duty to find each one of them a loving new home. However, I had been becoming more and more interested in complementary therapy and healing during my time there and there came a point when I knew that I needed to act on my instinct once again, leave and pursue this path. Spirit, it seemed, had other ideas.

One evening at home in my flatshare I told my friends that I intended to go into work the following day and hand in my notice. My plan was to complete my reflexology training and pay my rent through temporary work. I boldly executed the first part of this plan the very next morning, telling my surprised boss that I was handing in my notice with immediate effect. The sense of liberation was intoxicating. The world was my oyster (or so it felt). I just had to find myself a job with no stress to pay the bills, continue studying reflexology and then set myself free on my life path. I returned home that evening and jubilantly told my flatmates what I had done. Ciara said, "My sister's working on a contract at Kew Gardens and they're advertising for a new PR Manager. Why don't you apply?" Slightly annoyed, I explained that I was done with PR. If I was waking up feeling reluctant to go and do a job that most people in my profession would give their right arm for, what business did I have pursuing another job which was essentially the same? No: I was going to work on a supermarket checkout or as a receptionist until I passed my reflexology exams. Jacqui, who worked for the BBC, chipped in that she had some helpful insider knowledge on the yet to be broadcast fly-on-the wall documentary on Kew. She felt that it would really help me to stand out in an interview. No, I resisted. This was a nationally advertised position and there would be thousands of applicants. I would be wasting my time.

Two weeks later, I arrived at the Royal Botanic Gardens, Kew, for an interview. I did not want the job. Having prepared myself with loads of helpful snippets of insider information from the BBC and Ciara's sister, I promptly forgot them all. It was far and away the worst job interview I had ever had and I came out thinking, "Well, at least I gave it a shot." I could have fallen off my chair when, a few days later, I received notification that I had got the job. It was not a happy work experience for me and I managed a year in that position. It became clear to me later that I needed this time to really cement my ideas for the future. Plus, being in the undeniably stunning environs of the botanical gardens was a real privilege. In attempts to avoid the office politics I made regular trips round the gardens to gather interesting stories to use in press releases and during these walks I began to feel myself grounding and reconnecting with the earth. I also began to reconnect with Spirit and trust in my instinct once again. Thus far in my career I had experienced work with people (as a tour guide, in communications and recruitment), cities and large-scale communities (the American non-profit), animals (Battersea Dogs & Cats Home) and the earth (Kew Gardens). None of these jobs lit my fire and although I found a sense of purpose in animal welfare at Battersea, I was perplexed at the difficulty I found in sticking with a job for longer than a year or two. Looking back, I can see that a pattern was emerging. I was being prepared to recognise my purpose and to begin to apply all the experience I had gained to it.

Somewhere in between my work at Battersea and Kew, I became unwell. My GP ran some tests and told me that I was diabetic. This didn't feel right to me, and by chance a good friend's uncle was a leading UK diabetic consultant and agreed to see me. He immediately told me that diabetes was not my issue. The problem, however, was that nobody could tell me what the issue actually was. I decided to take matters into my own hands: I stopped drinking, smoking and eating meat. I told myself that if I missed any of these things after six months then I would revise my plan, but I had a strong feeling that I needed to cleanse my system, both physically and emotionally. In those days there did not exist the plethora of "clean eating" programmes we have now, so I just did what I felt was right. It was tough, but I'm good at challenges and within a few weeks I was already feeling a lot better.

As soon as this change was underway, I began to experience "happenings" again. One night, I was drifting off to sleep when I heard a loud rap on my bedroom door. I called out, assuming that one of my flatmates had come home a little worse for wear and wanted to chat. No answer. Two minutes later, there was another loud knock. This time I got out of bed and went to investigate only to find that both the girls were, in fact, still out. I was alone in the house. Slightly unnerved, I got back into bed. Five minutes later, I heard a deep, resonant male voice say my name very close to my right ear. Then another loud knock. I sat bolt upright in bed and said loudly, "Okay, that's it! You're frightening me! Please stop it and let me get to sleep." There were no further disturbances and I eventually relaxed enough to go back to sleep. It was at this time that I also began to feel the presence of a woman at home and it became so persistent that I broached it with Jacqui one evening. She confirmed that my description matched the owner from whom she had bought the property we lived in. She described her as a lovely, warm person who was happy to sell to Jacqui and her mum as she felt they would bring life and vibrancy to her home, which she was sad to leave. I like to think that she was revisiting her old home and liked what it had become.

The last few years of my twenties were a tumultuous time, full of doubt and chaos. Although my psychic development was very much shut down during this phase it is easy to see, years down the line, that this was a very important part of my learning. I turned thirty while living in the London flatshare and this seemed to mark an opening up of my consciousness to Spirit, to the extent that I told them that I was ready for the next phase of my life. I have always believed that we cannot be in a position to help anyone else until we have taken a good look at ourselves. When we are young, we make what we see as mistakes. Some of our choices seem poor or downright bizarre and it is necessary to wait for the passing of time before we come to realise what we have chosen to learn from that experience. Then, as we go forwards, we can impart that knowledge to others and our experience serves to help them in their learning.

Prompt: Has there been a period in your life when you struggled to see from a spiritual perspective? Have you lived with depression, addiction or were you just a party animal for a while, using "having fun" as an excuse to hide among the crowd and ignore your true purpose? Do you beat yourself up about this blip in your journey? Don't. Look for what you learned from the experience. There is always something.

Chapter 4

Fire and Air: My Irritating Soulmate

A soulmate is the... person whose love is powerful enough to motivate you to meet your soul, to do the emotional work of self-discovery, of awakening.
– Kenny Loggins

Shortly after turning thirty I announced to The Universe that I was ready to meet the man of my life. As the milestone birthday approached, I had visited two mediums in order to gain a sense of direction about my life, which felt out of control. They both seemed to assume that I was looking for love, which could not have been further from the truth. I had spent years in relationships that had been hard work. Four years on my own, although lonely at times, had felt like a holiday. The first psychic, Julia, was insistent that I was about to meet someone. She described hearing an ancient, "dead" language and told me that the man intended for me to meet had an Arabic influence in his heritage the same number of generations back as I had Jewish in mine (my great-grandmother was Jewish). She said she could see Gibraltar and felt that he had links with this place. This led to a series of hilarious coincidences. Having never met anyone from Gibraltar in my life I suddenly found myself bumping into men from Gibraltar all over the place. I have danced flamenco for many years as a hobby and at that time was attending various performances and parties across London. I would return from a night out and regale my flatmates with a story about yet another man from Gibraltar who I couldn't in a million years imagine being in a relationship with. Looking back, I'm so glad I trusted my own intuition in these cases. This is a prime example of how taking the information given to us by a psychic or medium too literally can backfire badly. If I had forced this issue, believing that I was "meant" to be with a Gibraltarian just because a psychic had told me so and because I was suddenly meeting them everywhere, who knows where I would have ended up? The guidance of a psychic or a medium is only as good as the translation they give you, and at times it can be very difficult to translate what we are seeing, hearing or sensing. It is up to the recipient of the information to take it on board, sit with it and just keep a quiet lookout for how that information might manifest to guide them in their life path.

The second psychic I consulted, Marco, read Tarot and insisted that I had in fact already met someone. I found this very frustrating as I had sought a reading with him in order to find out more about my path with healing but he wouldn't stop talking about my love life – or lack of it. "Are you sure you haven't met someone?" he kept asking, eventually qualifying it by saying, "You know when you stand next to someone every day at a bus stop and never notice them, and then one day they pick up something you've dropped and hand it to you and your eyes meet and you fall in love? It's like that."

One late autumn morning soon after that sitting and during my walk over the bridge to my job at Kew Gardens, I found myself chatting to Spirit. I had developed this habit since working at Kew as the walk from the station to the gardens was picturesque and I found it relaxing. To my utter amazement, I heard myself say, "Okay, I'm ready. Send him!" I stopped walking for a moment and waited, half expecting a man to rush over the bridge proffering me a bouquet of flowers, but Spirit clearly weren't prepared to act rashly on my demands. At home that evening, I told Jacqui and Leslie, who had spent many months gently trying to persuade me to try dating, that I felt that "The One" was around the corner.

Several weeks later, in early December, my good friend Helen invited me to a Christmas drinks party being thrown by her friend Nick. I had known Helen during my time at Warwick University but it was only in the years since graduating that we had become close friends. Nick was a university friend of hers whom I had never met, despite us all having been there at the same time. It was actually a running joke between us that I had never met "My Friend Nick". Finally, I was getting the chance. However, on the day of the party, I was coming down with a cold and had spent the afternoon dragging myself in and out of shops on Oxford Street, embroiled in Christmas shopping. I called Helen from the street. "Sorry," I told her, "there's no way I can make it tonight. I'm exhausted, I'm full of cold, my feet hurt and the last thing I feel like doing is socialising. I'm going to stay in and put my feet up with a cup of tea. You go with the others." Helen had also extended Nick's invitation to two of our other close friends, Sue and Jane. The four of us met regularly for dinner and drinks and supported each other through all sorts of escapades before we all gradually met partners and settled down. Helen told me that not only had Sue and Jane already cancelled, but Gary, her boyfriend, was an hour's drive away at his grandmother's house and it did not look like he would be back in time to go with her to the party. "Please come with me," she asked. "If it turns out to be rubbish I promise we'll just go and have dinner on our own." I agreed to go.

Hours later, standing in an immaculate bachelor pad in east London with a glass of champagne I couldn't drink because I had given up alcohol, I was starting to regret my decision. Bizarrely, almost every one of the party guests had been to university with me, but I didn't know a single one of them. The "*Surely* you must remember him/her" game was beginning to wear a bit thin as I repeatedly failed to recognise each guest as they arrived while Helen greeted them all like the old friends that they were.

My attention was caught by a small commotion by the door. A tall, dark and extremely handsome man had just made an entrance, and it had caused a stir. Before I could say anything,

Helen grabbed my arm and said, "Okay, you'll definitely remember this guy." She reeled off a list of impressive facts about him, none of which rang a bell. "Why on earth would I remember him?" I retorted rather uncharitably. "And anyway, he looks really arrogant!" Hardly had the words escaped my mouth when the tall, dark handsome stranger approached us and greeted Helen. She introduced us and I was appalled that he had the *chutzpah* to kiss me on the cheek (remember: I had been single for four years). She told him that I was studying reflexology and left us to it. I was fuming. Aside from the fact that most of the women in the room were staring at us, I assumed that his girlfriend must have accompanied him to the party and I didn't want to cause trouble. We chatted about reflexology and he offered to be a case study for my course. I barely concealed my sarcasm as I said, "Okay, I'll add you to the list." Throughout the evening Darius Norell couldn't have been more charming or attentive but, he claims, I swatted away every advance he made.

The following day I received a call from Helen. She was standing at a check-in queue at Heathrow Airport, waiting to board a flight. Hurriedly, she told me she'd had a call from Nick, asking whether Darius could have my phone number. Apparently he had insisted that Nick ask Helen to ask for it directly from me. "Why on earth does he want my phone number?" I asked. "Oh I don't know," Helen replied, "maybe he likes you and wants to get to know you better. For goodness' sake, I'm trying to get on a flight here. He's not an axe murderer; in fact he's a really nice guy. Just give him your number and go for a bloody drink with him!" She practically hung up on me. Truth be told, I was secretly impressed. When I was single in London, it seemed as if either everyone was too cool to invite another human being to exclusively spend time together or they just couldn't be bothered. It actually impressed me when Darius called that day to invite me to have lunch with him. My flatmates were beside themselves with excitement, as were some friends from work who had happened to come round that day. I was subjected to a barrage of questions about this mysterious man who had succeeded in breaking down my defences. As soon as I mentioned his name one of my friends said, "Hang on a minute: not Darius Norell?" I didn't even know his surname, but this friend went on to describe him in so much detail I asked her to stop – it was hardly a good precursor to a first date to know so much about someone before you'd even met them properly. Even more worryingly, it turned out that she knew all this because a friend of hers had dated him six months previously. This almost caused me to panic and back out, but I reminded myself that I had asked for this man to appear in my life and I needed to trust Spirit. In fact, this was the first of many bizarre "coincidences" linked to my meeting Darius.

Helped by the fact that he has an instantly recognisable name, I spent the following few months discovering that, apparently, half the people I knew were already acquainted with my new boyfriend. Several of my group of friends from university had known him. When we'd been together about six months, I was at a party for my goddaughter Isabella, Michelle's daughter, explaining this strange sequence of occurrences to Emma. We were just concurring what a wonder it was that we had never met before when we were joined in conversation by Michelle's sister-in-law, whom I have known for many years. Emma mentioned how happy I was with Darius. "Not Darius Norell?" she asked. She was a work client of his and had known him for years. This was getting ridiculous.

Darius and I have very different recollections of our first date: Sunday brunch in a small restaurant near where I was living in Clapham, South London. Incidentally, Darius also knew this restaurant because his sister was living several streets down from me at the time. We must have passed each other numerous times going up and down the main thoroughfare between the Commons in Clapham. Aside from the two of us, the entire restaurant was deserted. This was hilarious and embarrassing in equal measure as my flatmate Leslie had recommended the restaurant to me but told me to make sure we had a booking as it was almost always packed at the weekends. Following her instructions I had booked a table only to arrive to find my date standing in an empty restaurant chatting to the waiter!

Once we began to appreciate the rare privilege of dining together in an empty restaurant the date took on an ethereal quality: it was almost as if it had been closed especially for us and there were even strings of fairy lights looped over an indoor pergola to add to the romance. I chatted animatedly for a while and he showed me his new mobile phone, which had the exciting new ability to play music. During the demo it randomly started to play *The Scientist* by Coldplay which became our song and, later, Romy's too. Darius says I talked non-stop like a woman possessed throughout the whole lunch. I claim that he spent an inordinate amount of time staring at me and that I was forced to fill in the silences because he wasn't asking me any questions about myself. He says he didn't get a chance to ask anything. You can see the picture emerging here. One thing we both agree on: there was a moment, mid conversation/monologue, when we stopped dead and caught each other's eyes. I have never experienced a feeling like it. Darius has extraordinary eyes – I like to call them wolverine – and when I looked into them it was as if I could see into a past life. Momentarily, I found myself caught in a "remembrance" of a life in Egypt. I could feel the heat of candles, smell something like incense and feel the quiet reverence of a temple atmosphere. It was intense, and unforgettable. Remarkably, before I had the chance to say anything (I wasn't sure this was the kind of thing you could say to someone on a first date), Darius said, "You remind me of some kind of Egyptian princess." I emerged from that meeting feeling as if the world had turned on its axis. I called my parents and the first thing I said to my dad was, "I've met the man of my life."

Dad replied by telling me that he had also had a strong feeling about this relationship. It was two weeks before Christmas and when Darius arrived to spend the festivities with his family in Spain, he announced to them that he had met the woman he was going to marry.

It very quickly became apparent to me that Marco the tarot reader's assertions were correct. I might not have actually met Darius when I had that reading, but our paths had crossed a staggering number of times before we did meet. Firstly, we were at the same university for the same three years and had some friends in common. Mere weeks before the party at which we met, I had attended a first aid course as part of my complementary therapy training. It was in central London but I didn't know the area and got really lost looking for it. The venue turned out to be on the very road that Darius lived, directly opposite his flat. His sister lived several streets down from me and he visited her often. A month or two before we met I had bought tickets for a flamenco show but sold them back to the theatre at the last moment as I was committed to rehearsals for a flamenco show with my own group. Darius had tickets to the same show and admitted to me that it wasn't usually his thing but he had spontaneously felt like doing something different. Then there were the people who already knew Darius and had connections to me, and of course if you believe in past lives you could also say that we had known each other before, at least once, apparently in Egypt.

It wasn't long before I also worked out the meanings from Julia's sitting too. Half of Darius's family is of Persian extraction; his great-grandparents came from Tehran; his grandparents were immigrants to the UK and spoke Farsi at home, the ancient language that Julia could hear, but not place, during our sitting. My great-grandmother was Jewish, so she was absolutely correct in saying that he has an Arabic influence as far back in his family as I have Jewish in mine. And the Gibraltar link? I mentioned that he visited his family in Spain. None of them are Spanish but his grandparents moved out there fifty years ago and my mother-in-law still lives near Malaga. The first time he took me to visit, I experienced a revelation (and a small amount of relief) as he told me he had booked flights to Gibraltar, which was sometimes easier than flying direct to Malaga.

Experiencing a romantic relationship with a soulmate is not necessarily a permanently pleasant experience. After the initial euphoria of "finding each other" had faded a little, we found ourselves with a challenging union of opposites that provided us with a bumpy ride for some years. I used to joke when times were difficult that we were just getting all our most challenging stuff out of the way early on, to make way for a harmonious and solid relationship when things really got tricky years down the line. This turned out to be a far better prediction than I had ever thought possible.

Let's look at the term "soulmate". I'm fully aware that many interpretations exist and that one of the most popular espouses that we all have a singular soulmate: the other half of ourselves, without whom we are incomplete. While reading for my English Literature degree I discovered reams of poetry and prose waxing lyrical about the "perfect other"; the search for which doomed their authors to lives of despair. I prefer to think that every single individual soul in existence is inextricably linked to all the others. We are *all* "one". We all have a duty to live by the laws of the universe and in particular to live by love. Here on earth we can easily forget these laws and our lives become taken over by the desire to "find ourselves". What we often fail to realise is that the answer is very simple. We cannot necessarily find ourselves, or our soul's purpose, by following others' directions, by practising any form of spirituality or by travelling far and wide. As the saying goes, "Wherever you go: there you are." Nothing will magically make our problems go away. We find ourselves by loving ourselves, first and foremost.

If we spend our lives persistently searching for "the one" who will shower us with unconditional love and make life perfect, we are wasting our time. We are our own soulmate. We need to seek those with whom we can learn, and learning is often challenging. In the early days of my marriage a part of me found it disappointing that I had chosen a man who did not send me extravagant bouquets of flowers and make overt romantic gestures. I learned over the years that this is not what is important, and that this is not what *should* be important. When we decided to get married, I told him that I didn't want an engagement ring because I wasn't yet sure what kind of jewellery I wanted to wear on my finger every day of my life, and at that point it wasn't important; the importance lay in the fact that we were making a commitment to be together. Eleven years after we were married, he did buy me a beautiful ring and every day I look at it and love the fact that it represents the woman I became, thanks in part to my marriage. Our relationship is not in any way perfect; however, what I have learned from being with Darius has served me greatly, especially because it has sometimes been hard.

Some may find one individual with whom they have agreed to spend many years of discovery. For others of us, there may be several such "soulmates". Even when relationships are difficult and end acrimoniously, as was the case with me during my twenties, we can still ask, "What did I need to learn from this?" In my case, the answer did not come easily and I spent many years wondering why I had chosen to spend time with men who did not meet my needs nor respect my spirituality and who, in my opinion, had caused me pain through betrayal of my trust. Only later did I realise that these relationships were part of my learning process. By selecting men who at some point experienced addiction, I learned to recognise that trait in myself and use it to help me further on in my path when I chose to become a healer. Through these relationships, I learned, eventually, to recognise myself, to not expect a perfect union and to be realistic about the type of man I really needed to learn from and with. Experiencing these difficulties in my earlier relationships gave me the resilience I needed not to walk away from my relationship with Darius when we experienced early challenges; rather, it gave me the tools I needed to extend compassion and understanding towards him and myself and to trust my own instinct that we were, in fact, meant to be together.

Around a year into our relationship we experienced some real difficulties as we struggled to find a way to coexist together and blend our individually strong energies into a successful relationship rather than a constant clashing of opinions and beliefs. We were in our early thirties, my instinct told me that we were unequivocally meant to be together, possibly for the rest of our lives, and I also had a sense of how strong we would be as a couple when we learned to make our energies work together. In the meantime, however, we were clashing a lot. Both exceptionally strongminded people with a determination to blaze through life and leave our mark, we were also a little lost individually as we strove to find our footing. During this time and in an attempt to gain some clarity I attended a sitting at the College of Psychic Studies where I was myself sitting in development circle.

The only part of that sitting I recall concerns the medium's reference to my relationship with Darius at that time. She felt that it was in stormy waters, which was correct. She felt my exasperation, disappointment, fear and sadness that my partner seemed to be emotionally distant and wrapped up in his own issues. This was indeed how I felt, although of course there are two sides to each story. Suffice to say that at that period of time, Darius was wrestling with some important questions in his life and did not feel able to share this with me on an emotional level. Being such an openly emotional person, this hurt me deeply and I began to despair that our relationship could survive.

She went on to explain that she clearly saw Darius and I in a past life, in Medieval Venice. We were a young, successful couple in the city with a young child, a daughter. In this incarnation, we had the same roles as in this lifetime: he the husband, I the wife although in my understanding of reincarnation our gender can change from one life to the next; it is our soul, or our core being, that remains the same throughout all incarnations. I was a talented musician and fully immersed in Venetian musical culture, which I found enriching and fulfilling. Our marriage was happy and we had hopes for more children. However, this was not to be, as I was struck by a mysterious debilitating illness that would see me completely physically incapacitated, unable to play music again and in constant pain. I fell into a deep depression and felt I could no longer make sense of my life. Darius, as my husband, stood by me throughout, always by my side to care for me and for our child. The medium went on to explain that we had agreed between us that in this lifetime, I would spend a period of time being the supportive partner to my husband as he experienced a brief spell of discontent. She explained that it was helpful to my learning to provide support to a partner within a balanced relationship, just as he would do for me in return. This was in stark contrast to my previous relationship experiences, wherein I had felt that a lot of weight was on my shoulders.

Souls often do this; for example, if one soul has experienced suffering at the hands of another they often choose to reincarnate in reverse roles to balance out the karma of the situation and to increase their understanding of the human condition. In our Venetian life, Darius and I had chosen together for him to be the supportive partner. During this incarnation we had decided that I would try out the role of being the one to offer unconditional love and support during a testing time. Of course, what the medium did not see at that time and what now appears so obvious to me is that we would replay the original scenario again in this lifetime. Directly after Romy died, I became that woman again. I was depressed, mentally incapacitated, struggling to get through each day. Just like his Venetian self all those lives ago, throughout this time Darius was ever present and solid. He never gave up on me, even when I wanted to give up on myself.

As the quote at the beginning of this chapter states, "A soulmate is the... person whose love is powerful enough to motivate you to meet your soul, to do the emotional work of self-discovery, of awakening." This does not always come easily. Over the years, Darius and I have challenged and pushed each other but what has kept us both in a committed relationship is our combined quest for knowledge and purpose. At each difficult period we have eventually found our way back to each other and we ask, "What do we need to learn here? From the situation and from each other?"

I have always had pride in my forgiving nature but occasionally I have found it difficult to make peace after an altercation, or I have found myself carrying negative thoughts about another person if I feel they have treated me or someone I love unfairly. One of the most valuable lessons I have learned, I have learned from my husband. When we were first together and had a big quarrel, I froze him out for a day or two. I was so angry with him all I could do was to go over and over the ways in which he had hurt me. I imagined that he would carry on doing this because he was just so inconsiderate and self-centred and this led to me falling into self-pity, telling myself that this was typical; that I always ended up with men who treated me poorly, that this was all I deserved. You can see how quickly this type of thinking manifests into a lack of self-love. Eventually, he approached me and gave me a piece of advice that I often live by and which has made my life so much easier: "When you're faced with negative or angry feelings towards someone or something," he told me, "try doing the opposite to what you feel." Now, when we have argued, I remember these words and even if I think I could cheerfully throttle him, instead I give him a hug. It's amazing how good that feels! I have used this in many other situations and it is incredible how powerful it is to convert anger into an act of kindness. This is powerful learning, and I know it is one of the reasons why I have chosen Darius over many lifetimes.

I doubt that without the groundwork we put in early on in our partnership we would have survived the immense challenges we have faced in recent years. These have included of course the passing of Romy and the collapse of Darius's business partnership just weeks after she died and, later, one of our children's autism diagnosis. I chose a partner who communicates in very different ways from me but we have always sought to find a better way to communicate so that we can feel closer and take on challenges as a team. I am blessed with a lot of energy and passion and embrace change, which I do not fear. I trust my intuition and am not afraid to make impulsive decisions based on it. One of the traits I love most about Darius is his openness and willingness always to let me streak ahead and turn my spark into a flame. He supports my visions and my life in ways that I do not always recognise. And when my energy inevitably flags and I become despondent and doubting, it is Darius who pulls me up and points out to me the positives in the situation. To me, these characteristics are far more important than obvious romantic gestures and far outweigh all the little things about him that I find annoying. My natural inclination is to operate at a hundred miles an hour or so; Darius prefers to take things slowly. He's a morning person, I'm a night owl. I'm organised, he loses things. I do, he thinks. However, he was born under the astrological sign of Gemini, an air sign, and I find that this complements my Aries fieriness just as air fans flames. Darius provides the perfect amount of incentive to "fire me up" and I would say that I do the same for him. Ours is the partnership of equals that my father brought me up to seek in a marriage.

I am proud to say that this relationship, with all its

imperfections, has shown to me my true self. I have learned to be happy with myself, either in or out of my marriage. It has taken me many years, but with Darius's encouragement I have found my way to my calling as an author, a medium and a healer. When I started to write this book, his encouragement was boundless. I laugh as I recall a book dedication I read somewhere in which the author had written, "This book is dedicated to my wonderful wife and three amazing children, without whom this book would have been written ten years ago." This is not my experience. Darius has moved mountains and figuratively taken me by the shoulders and sat me down at my desk to write. Most of the time, I can see clearly why we chose each other and for this, I am thankful.

Prompt: In times of difficulty in your relationship, do you seek to "fix the problem" or do you try to reconnect, to build communication? What do you learn from your partner? Can you embrace your differences and turn them into powerful positive energy? What makes you stronger, as individuals and as a partnership? If you are not currently in a relationship, are you comfortable with yourself? Are you enough? What are you seeking in a potential partner? Are you being truthful about what best complements you?

Chapter 5

The Promise

What you seek is seeking you.
– Rumi

I was aware of the moment of conception for each of my four children and I knew that Romy was due to be born to us long before this point because I asked her to come.

In my work as a reflexologist I had chosen to specialise in fertility and pregnancy. I loved this focus; especially when I came to work with a woman both prior to and during her pregnancy and on to accompany her as she birthed her baby. I was privileged to perform this service for a handful of families more than once, which was truly special. Somehow, even before I had experienced pregnancy myself, I felt a deep affinity with this work and attended courses by many world-renowned leaders in this field. When newly pregnant with Kasper I travelled to America to study with Ina May Gaskin, author of the seminal work, *Spiritual Midwifery*. I was thrilled to participate in training run by the late, great Sheila Kitzinger, who also gave me tips on writing a book while operating as a full-time mother (she was herself a mother of five). I undertook doula training with renowned obstetrician Michel Odent and worked in the birthing centre of water birth pioneer Janet Balaskas and in the small team of Dr Gowri Motha and Yehudi Gordon. I did seek out these experiences, and yet at the same time I see that in some ways, they sought me. Although I no longer work in this field I acknowledge that for ten years of my life this played a very important part in preparing me for my future work and I feel that these giants of the birthing world were somehow placed in my path for me to learn from. I'm not just talking practicalities here: anyone can learn about the mechanics of conception and birthing. I mean the qualities that these individuals possessed which gave them their standing as highly respected, valued members of the world of pregnancy and birth. I studied these aspects well; noticing what it was about each one of them that made people sit up and listen: their dedication, their passion and their desire to help women in their care to empowerment.

At some point during this work I came across the book *Spirit Babies* by Walter Makichen, and this lead me to explore the avenue of what is known as "conscious conception". This is the idea that each child, or incoming soul, chooses its own parents in this lifetime and that there exists a contract between them that clearly lays out the learning for both parties. This applies to adoption, to good relationships and bad. Walter – a clairvoyant medium from the States who passed to Spirit himself in 2011 – claims to have been able to see the number of possible children for a woman or couple within the aura and suggested that the number of eventual children we have depends entirely upon two things: our free will to either offer or take up an invitation to parent a particular individual, and timing.

If you think this sounds kooky, I can tell you that I tested it out and I believe that it works. At the time that I encountered Walter's book, we were beginning to think about starting our own family. I was feeling a little impatient as, at thirty-four, I was well aware that the gap for being able to conceive was narrowing. In all honesty I would have had a child with Darius virtually from the moment we met, so sure was I that we were intended to be parents together, but he understandably felt that this course of action would have been a little rash. By January of 2008 he was still stalling a little due to the fact that we were essentially homeless. We had sold his flat in central London but had no idea where we should put down roots. We were living a nomadic existence sleeping in the spare rooms of various friends around London while we figured it out. We eventually found a flat to rent in Camden, North London, and shortly before moving day Darius was due to set off for a ten-day meditation retreat. This was the beginning of his enduring exploration of Vipassana meditation and Buddhist philosophy.

On the morning of his departure for the retreat centre in Belgium I went to use a fertility predictor test in the bathroom of the friend's home we were staying in. Having worked for years with women's health I was confident in my ability to read the body's natural fertility signals; I was using this test stick simply because a number of my clients were doing so and I wanted to check it out for myself to be able to better advise them. I was still half asleep when I looked at the results window, which clearly showed that I was ovulating. This woke me up: how was this possible on Day 6 of my cycle? For the uninitiated, a woman's average menstrual cycle is anything between 25 and 31 days. The time at which you are most likely to conceive is somewhere in the middle – around Day 15 of a 30 day cycle. Even with a cycle as short as mine, ovulation at or around Day 6, while not impossible, is highly unlikely.

Several months later, while training with Ina May Gaskin in the States I told her this story and asked for her view. Ina May was part of the original hippy trail of 1969 and spent most of her adult life living in the commune that eventually became The Farm in Tennessee. She told me something that fascinated me. She said that, with commune life, the menfolk often had to travel away to work for days or weeks on end. When a couple, or a woman, wanted to conceive it was not unheard of for this to happen at very random points in the woman's cycle, *when her partner was about to leave the commune for a period of time.* This seemed incredible to me, but what Ina May was essentially saying is that the woman's body is so finely tuned to welcoming a much-wanted baby that it can even tweak its own chemistry to enable a conception outside of the normal window. This certainly seems to have been the case for us.

On the day that Darius was travelling to Belgium I was working as a reflexologist and during that afternoon I was called to the home of a client, Bridget, who was about to birth her second child. I remarked as we began that it was a full moon that night. "I'll guarantee you're going to have this baby tonight," I told her. Any midwife will tell you that maternity wards are always more populated during full moons and thunderstorms. She drifted off to sleep during the treatment and as it came to an end I experienced a sudden dizziness, accompanied by the feeling that I was somewhere else. I didn't feel unwell in any way; more as if I had crossed a veil between two worlds, just for an instant. When I had finished the treatment Bridget woke from her sleep and immediately asked me if I was alright. Surprised, I told her yes. "It's funny," she said, "but just at the end of the treatment I had this really weird dizzy feeling but I felt that it was more to do with you than me." I joked that she was the pregnant one and reminded her of my prediction that her baby would arrive that night. I was right on that front, but it was another two or three weeks before I was to discover that she hadn't been the only pregnant one in that room.

As I reflected on this strange experience some months afterwards I became convinced that what we both felt, on some level, was the initial spark that would become our eldest son. I'm still not entirely sure how to explain what I think happened, but essentially I believe that my body allowed me to ovulate outside its normal window, right before Darius and I "said goodbye" as he left on a trip, and that almost twenty-four hours later I felt all the chemistry combine to create our first child. To this day, Darius still tells people that I conceived our eldest son while he was away in Belgium on a silent meditation retreat.

Kasper was a few months old when we began to think about when we might add to our family. I told a bemused Darius all about the conscious conception theory and we thought we would give it a try. There are all kinds of directives on how to invite your child or children to join you, but we thought it would be appropriate to use our own intuition and one evening focused our thoughts on whoever it was who was to be the next member of our family. Feeling a little silly, we talked to this soul and invited it to join us. Of course, conception, conscious or otherwise, requires a certain amount of physicality and I can say with all honesty that during it I felt an intense spiritual connection, the like of which I had never felt before. I can only describe it as feeling as if a third person had entered the room with us. Physically, I remember feeling a little dizzy and as if I were seeing stars. I knew, deep within me, that I had conceived but I said nothing to Darius. A few weeks later, while out with a friend, I remarked that I had to sit down while shopping as I suddenly felt very dizzy. It was a warm day and my friend commented that my dizziness was probably due to the heat. I almost replied, "No, it's not. It's because I'm pregnant!" Later that day I quietly took a pregnancy test that confirmed what I had intuitively known all that time: I was indeed pregnant.

And then there was Romy. In all the years I had worked with pregnancy I had often heard women talking about whether or not they felt they were "done" with childbearing. After Layla was born, I knew that I wasn't "done", but neither did I feel the overwhelming urge to have more children. However, as Layla grew up and started to move towards nursery school, rather than focusing my energy on my work path I found myself dreaming of adding to our family. As much as I loved my work and felt free to begin rebuilding my small business down in Sussex, I had a nagging feeling that our family wasn't complete. As time ticked past the nagging feeling grew more insistent and Darius and I fought bitterly over the issue, he arguing quite reasonably that we were fast approaching our forties, we had two beautiful, healthy children whom we adored, our financial situation could be better and another child would only stretch us further. All I could counter with was that I felt that someone was waiting to join our family. I could literally feel her presence, I knew she was a girl and I was getting increasingly desperate at Darius's resistance to opening the door and letting her in. "This is not just about me wanting another child," I kept telling him. "I'm telling you, there's another person waiting to join us; it's as if she's behind a closed door and I can't tell you how unbearable it is to me that you won't open the door to our child." It is rare for Darius to deny me something when I feel so strongly about it but on this he stayed frustratingly firm. No more babies.

Eventually, one night I made a promise to Spirit. "If you send me this child," I said, "I promise that I will give up my work with reflexology and birth and I will do whatever work it is that you want me to do. If you want me to work as a medium, I'll do it. If it's healing I'm supposed to be doing, I'll do that. Just please, please send me this child." I was truly in a place of desperation. Compared to major world problems, this seems like a ridiculous statement to make but, looking back on it now, I can see that I was obsessed with the idea of having a third child to the point that I almost lost all rational thought. It became the all-important focus of my life in a way that I never experienced with any of my other pregnancies. I've reflected on this a lot in the years since Romy passed, and although at the time it all felt very traumatic, I can see now that I was simply doing what I have always done: following the trajectory mapped out by my inner knowing, my intuition. I have become so adept at following this that when an obstacle – such as my husband's perfectly valid opinion, for example – gets in my way, it becomes catastrophic.

On a spiritual level, I believe that Darius knew how the situation would play out; not to the point that he was refusing to engage in it because he knew that Romy wouldn't stay with us for long, that's too conscious. I do believe that he was resisting the situation because on some level he knew the pain it would bring to us both. I, on the other hand, must also have been aware of the outcome on a spiritual level but I had blocked that out in favour of focusing on the learning we had to accumulate, and also on the strength of feeling between myself and Romy. Almost as if I had been allowed to remember a link from a previous life, the entire time I was lobbying my husband I could feel her presence very strongly. It felt like it does for me when I sense the presence of a person in spirit; it's confusing because it feels tangible, as if you could reach out and touch that person, but you can't see them in physical form. If you have children, imagine being able to feel their presence in the room or the house but not being able to reach out and hug them. That's how unbearable it felt for me during those months.

Towards the end of June 2013 we were visiting Darius's family in Spain. One hot afternoon we lay on sunloungers watching our children play with their cousins in the pool and a conversation occurred that I have never forgotten. Despite all the heated discussions we had had about the prospect of another pregnancy, I still couldn't let it drop. Risking the shattering of a peaceful afternoon, I broached the subject yet again. I went over my "closed door" theory again and sensed that Darius was slightly more receptive than he had been. In a moment of impulsiveness, I said, "Listen, I want to stop obsessing over the whole pregnancy thing and get back to getting on with our lives. Let's draw a line in the sand here. I'll make a deal with you: let's give this one shot. If I'm right, and this child is meant to join us, then I'll get pregnant on the first attempt, won't I? If I'm wrong, then that soul won't choose to join us and I promise I will never ask you about it again. If I don't get pregnant this month then I will let go of the whole idea and trust that my instincts were wrong." This gamble came with high stakes and I knew that I would have to deal with overwhelming disappointment if things didn't go as I hoped. On the other hand, the sense of liberation, at "walking my talk", on handing over to Spirit, was huge.

The following morning, Darius turned to me and said, "I'm really sorry, I know how important it is to you to have another baby and I thought what you said yesterday made a lot of sense, but I just can't do this. I can't explain why, but I can't." It took all my resolve not to blurt out, "It doesn't matter, because I'm already pregnant!" Once again, I had what I can only describe as a quiet sense of knowing. I *knew* beyond doubt that I had conceived again, and I was right.

I seemed also to have had a sense that Romy's presence in my life would somehow change its focus in a significant way. During my reflexology training, when asked to choose an area of speciality for my focussed project I was torn between fertility and palliative care. I have always been strongly drawn to what you might call the two ends of life: birth and death. A week or two before Romy passed I was chatting to Darius about all the logistics involved in my returning to work and before I knew what I was saying I told him, "You know, I have a feeling that when I do return to work after this maternity leave, I won't be doing this anymore." Darius was surprised, to say the least. I had spent a decade of my life living and breathing fertility, pregnancy and birth and here I was saying, "I really feel that I'm going to work with death and the dying!" As I said the words I was reminded of my struggle to choose my speciality over ten years previously and, as with other times in my life, I felt propelled along by words coming out of my mouth that didn't quite feel like I was saying them.

It would seem that a lot of different energies were realigning themselves in the immediate lead-up to Romy's return home to Spirit. Aside from my sudden change of direction over my work, Darius's business partnership was beginning to unravel in what would turn out to be a dramatic way. Our son was about to complete his first year of schooling and certain aspects were revealing themselves as being difficult for him. This prompted us to consider whether where we were choosing to live was right for him, and for us. Several weeks before Romy's death we found ourselves conducting a house hunt in several neighbouring towns and villages. We felt compelled to move our family closer to the inclusive, alternative city of Brighton and to place the children in a small independent school that we felt would be of enormous benefit. How to afford that school was a large question mark, but as it turned out, Spirit seemed to have that covered too.

Darius's Aunt Jeannette, his late father's sister, was a unique and fascinating person whom I loved instantly as she welcomed me so warmly into the family when we first met. A creative soul, she was always making art out of recycled materials and looking for new ways to engage with life. She did not suffer fools and if you caught the sharp end of her tongue you'd know about it, but she was a warm, engaging and bright woman and especially close to her nephew. After the births of each of our children she would always be keen to meet the new arrival but with Romy she was particularly persistent. Every time Darius spoke with her she would ask, "When on earth are you going to bring that baby to meet me?" At that time in her eighties, she found it more difficult to take the train from her home in London to ours in mid Sussex, so we agreed that we would make a trip to visit her at her apartment for the day. We packed all three children into the car and headed for London.

I recall very little detail about that day other than the fact that Romy slept for a lot of it and was fussed over by Jeannette. We made our usual trip to the gated garden in the square and then sat down to lunch together. Jeannette talked to us about the children's schooling and shared that she thought our lively, spirited pair would benefit from a less run-of-the-mill school. "If I had the money spare, I would give it to you so you could choose a really fantastic school for the children," she told us. This turned out to be something of a premonition as she passed shortly after that conversation. I like to think that she would have approved of the fact that her legacy to us allowed our children to attend the wonderful school that we found.

As we were leaving that afternoon I went to say my goodbyes

to Jeannette and, as I did, a strange feeling came over me. I recall us looking into each other's eyes in a way that we had never done before, and somehow the word "goodbye" seemed to have a deeper resonance than normal. I did not say, "See you soon," as I usually did, and as I watched Jeannette's elegant, upright yet frail figure receding back into her doorway I felt a wave of intense sadness. I almost turned to Darius and said, "I don't think we're going to see her again," but I stopped myself. A week or two later, as we arrived in Spain for a family visit, we heard the news that Jeannette had passed quietly in her sleep. Apparently, she had visited her local hospital a day or two beforehand to tell them that she felt unwell, but was turned away. I have always believed that she had a sense of her impending passing, which was why she was so insistent about meeting Romy, and why we experienced that odd exchange as we said goodbye. Just nine days later, Romy joined her. I have often wondered whether there existed a contract between them. Perhaps it was intended that they meet in earthly form before they returned back together. Perhaps Romy had something to teach, or to learn from her great-aunt.

The message of this book hinges on the idea that we can live our lives more positively by adopting the belief that we choose our path in this life before we are born. It suggests that we choose all the pitfalls, wrong turnings and difficult interactions and that we choose this way because we want to learn. The more challenges we put in our path to encounter, the more learning we experience and the better that will serve us when we return home to the spirit world.

So let's suppose that our connection to Spirit is in place when we arrive into this world and it continues throughout our time here on earth. Why do we not remember it from the outset? Because it does not serve us or our intended life purpose to have full memory recall of the spirit world we come with only the faintest connection to it in order that we may make mistakes and learn from our experiences before we return home. There are many documented cases of children who appear to have retained memory of past lives in intricate detail, including information that they could not possibly have known, so perhaps it is possible that we may be born into our current incarnation with access to memories of the other side, and to other lives. There is, however, also a view that life on the other side – or heaven, as some wish to call it – is so beautiful that if we were born with memories of it we would simply want to return straight away. Our earthly environment somehow manages to all but erase anything other than suggestions of life in the spirit world to ensure that we carry out our earthly existence in full and access the learning we agreed to take on.

During our time here we can learn to strengthen our connection to Spirit; not to sidestep the learning part in any way but to make a little more sense of the world around us, to remind ourselves that our loved ones are always with us whether they are in this world or the next, and to inspire us with our life purpose. With all the negative events happening around us out of our control, I find it immensely reassuring to think that the Spirit world "has our back"; that there is always someone or something there for us, even during our darkest moments. Having lived through devastating trauma myself I know that I would rather live my life with a belief that there is help and hope for a better future rather than drowning in my own misery and despair.

I appreciate that to many suggesting that we can have conversations with Spirit, or even with our deceased relatives, sounds ludicrous but I have been doing it my whole life, and the older I get, the more convinced I am by the results that I have. To anyone reading this who thinks it's still poppycock, I invite you to try it. Whenever you encounter a hurdle in life, large or trivial, try "talking" to Spirit in your head and ask the question you need an answer to. I have found that as long as the question is posed with the best of intentions then you will rarely be met with silence. When my maternal grandmother was in very poor health and my mother was struggling to know how best to care for her and give her what she needed in her final weeks and months, I suggested that she try asking her late father for help. For several nights, she told me, just before she fell asleep she sent out a thought to her father, to whom she had been very close in life, and asked him to please guide her to whatever was best for my grandmother at that time. My parents had spent months agonising over whether it was the right choice to place my grandmother in a care home and whenever they tried to search for one they found only places that, for one reason or another, simply didn't feel right. Within days of my mother asking for help from Spirit, they took a detour while out driving one day and stumbled upon a beautiful rest home seemingly out of nowhere. They thought it would be full but there was just one place available. To all of our amazement my grandmother was happy to go there and spent the last months of her life being cared for lovingly by nuns in a place full of beauty and grace.

There is no doubt in my mind that not only can we all have a dialogue with Spirit if we so choose, but also that our lives operate according to the contract that we prepared before we are born into this life. Alongside the many books I have read on this subject, I also have countless examples from my own life. The key is to listen and to always be ready to pay attention, even to signs and symbols that may not immediately seem relevant. We live in a world that demands results – and quickly. We require everything to be visual, obvious and formulated in such a way as to fit in with our particular preconceived ideas. This may explain why some people are bitterly disappointed with psychic readings where they have been told about their career path instead of their love life, or why others may dismiss a medium as of poor standard simply because they went for a sitting wanting to speak with their father but instead received a communication from their great-aunt, to whom they were not close. The lesson here is that, sometimes, the information is more important than the messenger. As much as we may desperately miss a particular loved one, it is not guaranteed that he or she will turn up to a medium just when we ask them to. However, if we ask for their help, or for a sign that they are around us and then *we pay attention to receiving*, then we may be astounded at what happens.

My "bargain" with Spirit all those months previously had clearly been effective as Romy was very quick to join us. I do not believe that this was merely coincidence. Contrary to what many people believe, when you consult any psychic you walk away from that sitting with free will. This means that whatever that psychic or medium has told you, it is information they have received either by reading your energy or by forming a link with Spirit and translating it accurately enough to assist or guide you on your life path or provide evidence of survival after death. A practitioner operating with only your highest good in mind will never, ever instruct you to act on anything they tell you. As I have said, on occasion something comes up that makes no sense whatsoever to the sitter, and it is only sometimes weeks or months down the line that a missing piece falls into place and the information makes sense – remember that man from Gibraltar I thought I was going to meet?

Prompt: Have you ever considered the possibility that there has been a "contract" in play in your life? Who was, or is, involved? How has it played out? Do you feel empowered by it, or hard done by? If you are a woman with biological children, were you aware of the moment of conception? Did you dream about your children before you conceived them, or during pregnancy?

Chapter 6

Something About Romy

Important encounters are planned by the souls long before the bodies see each other.
– Paulo Coelho

Almost every parent thinks their child is special and I can say unequivocally that I have felt this in one way or another about all of our children but there really was something about Romy. Since she left us I have read many accounts written by mothers whose children have passed and it appears to be a common phenomena that some of them noticed a particular child as special or different in some way, or in some cases that they had a distinct "knowing" that their child would not grow up in this world. "I looked at him the day he was born and I just knew he wouldn't be with us for long" is an example of a recurring sentiment. Another is, "She was just so perfect, so beautiful a person that I knew that she wouldn't be staying." Hearing someone tell us, "God needed another angel in heaven," can be one of the cruellest sentences we can hear in our newly bereaved state and yet according to these anecdotes many children and young people who pass to Spirit before they reach adulthood do seem to possess some kind of otherworldly quality that marks them out from others.

I can't say in all honesty that I felt this consciously about Romy, but there were some pointers. Of course, hindsight is a marvellous thing and can also prove very convenient when applied to things told to us by psychics and mediums, but these indicators came to me in person, both before her birth and after her passing as well as later through various mediums and psychics. Like much of the information I share in this book, the fact that there has been so much crossover has really served to cement their authenticity for me, especially at times when my faith in Spiritualism has been ebbing. One meeting with a medium finally corroborated what I had felt for so many months: there was someone waiting to join us. However, the way in which this information was delivered seems to me today to be another indicator that perhaps Romy's stay here in this lifetime was always going to be special in some way.

Growing up, I occasionally visited psychic fayres with my parents and it was a pleasant way to pass a Sunday afternoon. Nowadays I sometimes enjoy bringing my own children to browse the crystals and listen to the Tibetan singing bowls. One rainy afternoon I stumbled across a flyer for a local event but unusually for me I was a little lacklustre about going. I was tired from running around after the children and although I would normally have leaped at the opportunity to spend a quiet hour or two browsing by myself, this time I wasn't feeling it. I was in the middle of mentally listing numerous domestic tasks that should be taking precedence when I suddenly felt a strong urge to get in the car and go. I recognised that this was Spirit telling me that there was a message waiting for me, but still I was reluctant. "I'll go, have a cup of tea, buy a crystal and come home again," I told myself.

When I arrived, I wandered aimlessly around the hall until I came to the small tables where the mediums and psychics had set up their stalls. There were around six in total and all but two were engaged in sittings. I looked over at the two unoccupied mediums. The first was a woman around my age who seemed friendly, open and pleasant. The second was a man whose appearance, I can't lie, didn't exactly draw me in. A large, heavy-set man, bald, with tattoos and piercings and an apparent inability to look you in the eye; to be completely honest I felt myself recoil a little as I passed him. I circled the hall and decided that I would go and sit in front of the warm, open-looking woman and see what she had to say. What happened next really gave me a jolt. I literally felt hands on my shoulders – actual hands; I could feel an imprint, the energy, the pressure of fingers and even some warmth. I spun around in shock to see who was holding on to me but of course there was nobody there. These hands guided me strongly and very purposefully towards the male medium and sat me down in the chair opposite him. Imagine my embarrassment! I almost blurted out, "I'm sorry, there's been a mistake, I didn't actually want to see you, I wanted to see her!" but I was far too polite for that and instead smiled sheepishly and waited to see what would happen next. I was reeling from what had just happened, not to mention mortified at the prospect of having to sit through a reading with a medium who I did not feel in the least bit drawn to. I learned an emphatic lesson from Spirit that day, in trusting their guidance and of never judging by appearance.

That sitting turned out to be a memorable one for its accuracy. Eddie was kind, engaging and immediately made a connection with my late grandmother Sylvia who proceeded to give piece after piece of information about my life. He even gave me the initials of my children's names and told me in no uncertain terms that I was meant to write a book and that I should jolly well get on with it.

As much as all the information was helpful to me – and in some way, exactly what Spirit wanted me to hear at that time – the burning question I had was of course whether I would have another baby. Considering how far up in my consciousness it was I was amazed that Eddie didn't give any mention of it whatsoever. I felt my spirits start to sink, my inner voice telling me that I wasn't hearing any information about it because it wasn't going to happen. As the sitting came to an end I waited for him to ask me if I had any questions, but he didn't. As I prepared myself to leave I found my voice. "I have a question," I stated. The look on Eddie's face told me that he knew I was going to ask a question and that he was distinctly uncomfortable with it. I ploughed ahead anyway. "Can you tell me if I'm going to have another baby?" I asked.

I knew from my own training all those years ago that I was treading on tricky ground. As a medium, it's always difficult to comment on pregnancies for reasons that I now completely appreciate. Eddie answered me so quickly that he practically overlapped the end of my question, standing abruptly and packing away as he did so. "You'll have another girl," he said bluntly. I was so euphoric to hear that information that I failed to notice the way he delivered it; reluctantly, and with distinct discomfort. I would go as far as to guess that he received information about Romy earlier on in the sitting and quite rightly chose not to give it to me. He knew that I was going to ask the question as he could sense how much it was overshadowing my life at that time. Before I had even finished asking it, he was responding. He must have realised that I had asked the question because I wanted to have another child and yet he delivered the reply so tersely. There was a complete absence of any accompanying information that usually goes along with such happy news, such as, "I see daffodils: you'll have a girl in the springtime." He had connected with my grandmother so convincingly and yet he also failed to tell me that this baby would be born three days before her own birthdate – a piece of information that I know that she would have revelled in telling me as my own birthday falls the day after hers and this was always very meaningful to her.

In essence, I believe that I was drawn to that sitting for several reasons. Some of the information I was given was relevant to my spiritual path in life, and I think that by giving that information, Spirit was gently planting a seed that would serve me in my darkest times ahead. I have always felt that there are certain things we are not supposed to be party to. Imagine if I had been told, either by Eddie or directly by Spirit, that Romy was not going to be with us for very long. What would I have done?

I can imagine one or two decisions I could have made which could have dramatically and irrevocably altered my life path because, medium or not, I am human and any person would go to extraordinary lengths to avoid experiencing the death of their own child. I could have taken a decision that denied Romy the chance to come here and experience the life lesson she had chosen, and one that Darius and I had explicitly agreed to be a part of. What then? In the deepest throes of my grief something that saved my sanity on numerous occasions was reminding myself that this is a human experience.

I constantly returned to the quote from Pierre Teilhard de Chardin: "We are not human beings having a spiritual experience. We are spiritual beings having a human experience."

Just days after Romy passed and while our children slept in our home in the care of our parents, Darius and I went for a walk at dawn. We sat down in a dew-drenched field on what promised to be a hot July morning and we asked ourselves, "Why did this happen? To us? To her?" We talked for hours about the possible spiritual reasons why all three of us had chosen things to be this way. On a spiritual level it made perfect sense: we had a contract. Perhaps Romy chose Darius and I because we are people with unconventional spiritual beliefs and because neither of us is afraid to stand up and speak about those beliefs to others; not in a preachy way, but in the way of sharing the insights we have gained which we feel would benefit others.

Why would Eddie not have told me what was going to happen so I could choose not to go ahead and get pregnant? This is a big question, and a reasonable one. In the worst days of my loss, when the pain at missing my daughter was so intense it felt physical, I asked myself this over and over. I didn't just question Eddie's decision, but my own abilities. Why, when I had always had such a strong link to Spirit, would they let me go ahead and do something that would cause me such pain? The only conclusion I could draw was that I had somehow chosen this, along with Romy and Darius, for some higher purpose that I am not privileged to know in this lifetime.

Very late on the night of 17th July I had called Michelle – the close childhood friend to whom I had described my very first spiritual experience so many years ago – from King's College Hospital. I have no recollection of our conversation at all but she tells me that in the middle of explaining all the tests and theories the hospital were working on, I suddenly broke off and wailed, "I knew this was going to happen!" Michelle asked me gently what I meant and apparently I said something like, "I just knew this was going to happen. She's too perfect! There's no way she was going to be able to stay!"

A week after Romy left us, Michelle dropped by to visit. After her brush with Spirit through my childhood experience she had gone on to become just as interested in Spiritualism as I am and over the years we have had many fruitful conversations, often long into the night, about our beliefs. Along with Emma, she is a much-trusted sounding board for many of my spiritual thoughts and over the years we have shared some extraordinary experiences. We always seem to know exactly when to contact each other and are very often "tuned in" at important times in our lives. Like the true friend that she is, Michelle had made a long drive after a day at work just to come and sit with me and offer to help with the children. I was still all over the place and welcomed her presence in the house as it allowed me to switch off for a while.

Minutes after Michelle's arrival we were in the kitchen making a cup of tea when, out of nowhere, she told us that she had been talking to her friend Jan about us. I had never met Jan but had heard Shelley speak about her and knew that she was a medium. Shelley explained that she wasn't sure why but she had felt compelled to tell Jan about our situation and ask whether she had any sense of why Romy had not been destined to stay with us. In an extraordinary email exchange, Jan's reply to Shelley had exactly described the theories that I held, most of which I hadn't shared with a soul. Bearing in mind that the only information previously known to Jan was that Michelle and I were lifelong friends and that Darius and I had just lost our baby daughter whose conception had been very fast, here is what she wrote:

It sounds as if Ali and Darius together were a channel to release Romy back home on a much, much higher spiritual plane than most spirits. Some souls just need to collect something special to place into their aura to help them on to a new soul journey. This only needs to take a short while in physical human form, which, in Romy's case, it did. They call it a kind of collective consciousness but the soul who chooses to make such a journey will have to choose its accompanying helper souls very carefully and wisely, and both Ali and Darius are extra special. Together they possess the mixture of a perfect essence Romy needed for her ongoing journey. They should feel honoured to have been part of this special transformation for Romy. They will be greatly rewarded on a karmic level, which they probably know already. When their time comes, Romy will use that special essence to take them to a much higher level of consciousness, where they belong. In the meantime, they both need to focus on as much light as they can get in order to fill the gaps that have been left from this transferring of light.

By this I mean that Romy has used up some of Ali's and Darius's special "light essence" which she will in turn use to help other souls. This then leaves Ali and Darius with chunks missing from what's left. This would have been part of their soul contract and the big test is happening around them now with regards to replacing that light. It is some people's mission to go into a darkness in order to find the light. You can't always see the light in the light, but you can see it in the darkness.

I feel that Ali and Darius conceived Romy very quickly exactly because of this spiritual contract and corresponding spiritual link between them all. Romy came to them because all three were perfectly ready for this transfer of light energy. Now, Ali and Darius both need to receive healing from other special light workers instead of giving. That's another important learning process for both of them too – learning to receive instead of giving all the time!

If I can be of any help please let me know. I have retired from all my healing and reading work but I do make exceptions when special souls need a hand.

I still read these words occasionally and am always astounded at how a new meaning will reveal itself as time unfolds. I can see now, for instance, what Jan was referring to by all the talk of "going into the darkness" when I think back to the extraordinary chain of events which took place around us just after Romy's death – in particular the sudden ceasing to be of Darius's business partnership. Caught in the middle of this maelstrom, we asked ourselves more than once why on earth we seemed to have been singled out for blow after devastating blow at a time when we could hardly cope with life. Jan's words are helping me even now to understand how we choose our path in this lifetime to gain maximum learning before we return to Spirit, and that sometimes, the best learning is through facing difficulty.

I could tell that Michelle felt bad about having essentially set us up to meet with Jan at such an early stage in our grief without having asked us first, but as always her instincts were spot on. My immediate response to her reading of Jan's email was to ask, "When can she see us?" To my surprise Darius, usually a little more reserved in such situations, enthusiastically agreed that he would also love to see her.

And so it was that we found ourselves sitting in a light, airy and spacious living room in Kent in front of a stunning array of glass bottles filled with coloured liquids. To those of you familiar with Aura-Soma, these bottles were very similar, but were Jan's own interpretation of this particular divination tool. Jan asked us each to pick five bottles and she then proceeded to talk us through each of our choices, interpreting and explaining the colours and their meanings and then expanding this to form a link with Spirit and give additional information.

She reiterated what she had said in her email and told us that she had a clear image of Romy, who was with a woman whom, she thought, had been a nurse during her time on this earth. This woman was wearing what looked like an old-fashioned nurse's hat: white and starched so that the corners stuck out. My grandmother Sylvia was a nurse during the war years but the description Jan went on to give didn't quite match her character. This lady was to come up again during another completely unrelated sitting. I still have trouble placing her and so I can only assume that she could be a family member who I am not aware of, or perhaps a guide. I have also begun to wonder whether she might be the woman I describe as a "midwife" who accompanied Romy when I "saw" her while having a facial. The headgear is strikingly similar.

The part of that reading that has stayed with me the most concerns a question I asked Jan right at the end of our session. I told her about an incident involving a column of intense blue light that I had seen at Romy's grave and which I describe in detail in Chapter 11. I did nothing more than describe how it looked; deliberately not giving any information about how it made me feel, the tangible shift in energy it had brought about or any theories I had drawn myself. Straight away she said, "I'm being given the information that this was your soul group you encountered. This is a collection of souls with whom yours resonates very strongly, and somewhere in among them will have been Romy's. They wanted to reassure you that you are not alone on this earth. None of us are ever alone. You have chosen a lonely path to walk and they took the opportunity to appear to you and reassure you that all will be well, that they are always with you." At no point had I told Jan that I had heard a voice saying, "All is well. We are with you." Neither had I conveyed that I felt a sense of familiarity; that the column of light felt like a collective and that I thought I could feel Romy's presence among them. What she was saying seemed to fit with such striking accuracy that it almost took my breath away.

Jan was a wonderfully warm and caring woman who genuinely wanted to offer her help. I was so glad that we had arrived at her home with a huge bunch of flowers for her as she wouldn't take a penny from us and gave us a whole morning of her time, for which we were extremely grateful.

When I think back, admittedly some of the time through rose-tinted glasses, I recall so many people reacting to Romy in a way that seemed unusual. To us, of course, she was perfect and worthy of our adoration but it struck me just how many times I was stopped by strangers: in the supermarket, on the street, who commented on her alarmingly blue eyes. It was if she somehow connected to people with her eyes. She held your gaze and it was like looking into two pools of cool blue deep water. It was mesmerising. Strangers would at first coo over her just as they might over any other baby but as soon as they saw her eyes they would become almost delirious with admiration. This happened numerous times and it only contributed to my feeling that there was something spellbinding about my youngest daughter.

When Romy was a newborn I couldn't "see" anything about her future life or personality traits. Let me explain. When Kasper was a few days old, I had a clear image on my "screen" one evening while sitting with him. I saw him with horses, and I saw him with a guitar. I shared this with Darius, telling him that I truly believed that our eldest son would have a real affinity with animals and that he would also have a gift for music. Despite having a very musical grandfather I do not play an instrument and can't claim to have any musical ability other than a love of listening to it and a passion for flamenco dance that has endured for twenty years. Darius, likewise, does not possess much musical ability (although he rather likes to think that he does!). I felt strongly from the very beginning of his life that Kasper would have an exceptional ear for music, and this was reinforced by a very odd encounter I had in an esoteric shop in Covent Garden, London.

I had specifically gone to visit Equinox Astrology to have a birth chart drawn up professionally for Kasper. Astrology is not something I profess to know very much about and I'm certainly not someone who reads their daily forecast but I have always been fascinated by the idea that personality traits might be governed by the position of the planets at the time and place of our birth. Professionally astrology goes much further than declaring someone to be fiery just because they were born under the sign of Aries. For a start your birth sign, or sun sign, is just one of numerous pointers in your astrological birth chart and in fact your opposing, or moon sign, often gives bigger clues to the person that you are. In any case, I was keen to have a chart drawn up for my new son and interested to read about what might lie in store for us as parents.

As I went to collect the chart I had Kasper, then aged around six months, with me. As he handed me the chart, the man stopped for a moment and looked intensely at Kasper. "Do you mind my asking," he said, "whether this child's father is English?" Kasper does look very much like Darius, whose dark good looks are influenced by his Persian heritage, but at this stage I would have said that he didn't look particularly un-English at all. Plus, Darius was born in England to two British-born parents and always identifies as such, so I truthfully answered that no, his father was British. "Why do you ask?" The astrologer paused and then replied, "It's just that when I was drawing up his chart I could hear other languages; one of them quite unusual.

I have a very strong feeling that if neither you nor your partner speaks another language at home then your son will have a real talent for this." I had heard this reference to an "unusual" language before, during the sitting with Julia. She claimed to hear snatches of Farsi, the old Persian language spoken by Darius's grandparents. It was extraordinary to hear this said about my six-month-old son. The astrologer went on, "It's not just languages, he'll have an exceptional ability for mimicry of all kinds; he has a finely-tuned ear."

Well, this turned out to be completely accurate. My oldest boy has a deep affinity with animals of all kinds (I have yet to test my horse theory further) and is one of the best mimics I have ever heard. He has an uncanny ability to copy anyone's intonation, phraseology and linguistic idiosyncrasies. You might argue that with two parents who speak four additional languages between them in addition to English then this would be a given; but is it? Kasper's "finely-tuned ear" extends to a real gift for music, as I predicted. Like my maternal grandfather, Bert, he is able to pick up a hitherto unknown instrument and get some kind of pleasant noise out of it. Within weeks of picking up an electric guitar and after just four weekly lessons he was picking out the correct chords to strum along to Elvis' *Blue Suede Shoes*. I admit to being envious of his talent.

When Layla was a few days old I received an image that clearly depicted her with paintbrushes, pencils and all kinds of art equipment spread about her. She had unruly hair and a real feeling of free-spiritedness around her and her fingers were stained with paint. I knew she would have a love of art and again I was right. Layla is a true observer; quieter than her brother before her but watching everyone and everything. She loves nothing better than to mess around making marks on paper with some kind of art materials, is constantly covered in paint and goes her own way with everything she does.

With Macsen, I felt that physical activity and sports would

be his focus and so far this is playing out. While pregnant with him I had an overwhelming feeling that I was carrying a boy, that he would be big, strong and sporty and I had an image of him being the kind of person who enters a room and brings the light in with him. At the age of two, Macsen was obsessed with footballs and has a really strong boot on him. With a birth weight of almost 10lbs he was by far the biggest of all our babies and he is a full-on, full pelt type of boy, always looking for activity. And when he walks into a room, he is like pure golden sunshine. Coming as he did after the devastating wrench of losing Romy, there was always a sense of healing and hope about him, but when I think about his future I see him surrounded by adoring people, being the type of person always invited to parties and lighting up everything around him.

Romy was different. I realised within a couple of weeks that I hadn't had that familiar feeling that I'd experienced with both our older children and I tried to make some things fit. I imagined her being an accomplished writer, of having an ability with small children but I knew that these images were flat as I had created them with my mind. I didn't want to admit it to myself but I knew that I wasn't getting that "spark" from Spirit that I was so used to in my daily life. I told myself that it was probably because I was so tired and consumed by having three preschoolers and that it would come back when I found time to make the space for it.

Just two weeks before Romy left us, I remember very well a quiet afternoon spent just the two of us at home before we walked up to the village to collect Kasper and Layla from nursery and school. I had fed Romy, she had slept peacefully while I read, and after she woke I changed her and played with her for a while on the sofa. It was a hot day so I had left her in just her nappy. She had just learned to roll and was delighting in flinging herself from side to side while I tried to kiss her little belly. We were both laughing and I couldn't stop looking into her eyes. I remember that I said to her, "I just love you so much! Thank you so much for coming here and for choosing me as your mummy. What would I do without you?" This is a moment frozen in time and torn with conflicting emotions. On the one hand, it's a beautiful memory of a perfect time spent with my daughter, laughing and playing. On the other, it's a chilling memento of the fact that just two weeks later I would be forced to put those words to the test in the most brutal way. I would live to see just what I would do without her.

Prompt: Who are the meaningful people in your life? Have you told them? Do you make time to think about how they enrich your life and in what ways could you enrich theirs?

Chapter 7

The Contract

We have soul contracts with every person in our lives to live in the vibration of truth.
– Molly Friedenfeld

Thursday 17th July 2014 started out like any other normal day. We'd been enjoying a very hot summer, which anyone who has ever lived in England will know is both a rarity and a joy, and it was nearing the end of the school summer term. Kasper was just coming to the end of his first year at school in the local primary and Layla, nineteen months younger, was leaving our village nursery, which filled me with nostalgia as it had become so familiar to us over the four years we had lived in the village. I was still learning to juggle the logistics of getting three children ready in the mornings before dropping the older ones off at two separate venues. I was grateful for the warm weather as at least that meant we didn't have to wrestle with scarves, gloves and coats. In the midst of the chaos of teeth brushing, packed lunch making and general scrabbling about, I popped Romy into her pram in just a vest with a light cloth blanket over her and we set out on our walk to school, and then nursery.

On the way back down through the village I noticed that Kasper had left his water bottle in the basket of the pram. It was such a hot day and I worried that he wouldn't think to visit the water fountain at school enough so decided to walk back round to school and drop it off for him. That walk is forever emblazoned on my memory. During it, I chatted to Romy, who was awake, smiling and gurgling in the pram. I often wittered away at her during our walks and enjoyed seeing her reactions. However, this morning, for some reason I wasn't pointing out birds, trees and flowers or singing. I was having a serious chat with her, and to this day I don't know why, or how, those words came to me but I remember them as if they had been burned on to my mind.

"Do you know," I began, "I really had to fight with Daddy to get you here and I know that you were waiting for a while to come. But I made a promise to Spirit. I said that if they sent you to me, I would do their work. So when Mama's ready to start back at work, that's what I have to do. I have to do Spirit's work, I have to read for people and do healing. No more reflexology and doula work for me!" I can remember the exact spot on the road that I was when I made that statement. If ever I have occasion to pass it now, which is rare, the hair stands up on my neck and I feel chilled to the bone. I feel that this "conversation" (as much as you can have a conversation with a four-month-old baby) was a pivotal moment in my understanding of the situation and it somehow unlocked the permission Romy needed to leave. Hours later she was unconscious and the next day she had gone. I know on a deep level that hearing that confirmation was the signal she needed that we had reached the point in our soul contract where she was free to return home to Spirit. The events to come were set out on a stage, and various other players all had their parts too.

We got home and I decided to drive over to the neighbouring village to a café that we'd never been to before. We had already made the decision to move the children to a small independent school in Brighton and were considering a house move slightly closer to it. I placed Romy in the back of the car in her car seat and as we drove off up the road I said, "Well, Romy, this is our last day together." I have described this day in some detail in the prologue to this book, and as I mentioned there, when I said these words I was referring to the fact that this was the last day we would have on our own together before the summer holidays began. I had been so looking forward to the long stretch of summer ahead with my three children and we had made detailed lists and plans of all the activities we wanted to do and all the favourite places that Kasper and Layla wanted to share with their new baby sister.

The café is situated next to a beautiful florist and was on that day perfectly shady, underpopulated and relaxed. I settled down there with Romy, emailing Darius with one hand while ordering coffee and food and pulling faces at Romy. We sat, I ate, we sang, we laughed and I showered her with kisses.

Laughter distracted me from our bubble and I noticed a woman with a boy and a girl, aged around eleven and nine, enter the café. I tend to notice people and details and something about this woman made me keep looking. She was tall and statuesque with red hair and wearing a green summer dress with a tropical print that seemed very appropriate next to the hothouse blooms of the florist. She was very chatty with the café owner and spent several minutes while waiting for her coffee exchanging pleasantries and laughing with her. As she exited with her children they passed our table and her daughter stopped and stared at Romy on my lap. "Mummy, look at the baby! She's so beautiful, look at her eyes!" she exclaimed, causing the whole group to stop by our table. I smiled hello and was struck by the fact that her son – whom I would have thought was far too cool to have been bothered by a small baby – was equally charmed by Romy. They couldn't seem to stop looking at her and were rooted to the spot, drinking her in. Eventually, we all smiled indulgently at each other and they went on their way.

That woman is also etched on to my memory, but not just for the reasons you may think. She came to represent to me something I still have trouble explaining or reconciling with my logical mind.

After Romy seemed restless and uncomfortable and with the creeping feeling that something wasn't quite right, I packed up our things, placed her gently back into her pram and we left for the car. We passed a small supermarket on the high street on our way towards the car park and I dashed in quickly for some water for our journey home. As I was standing in the queue for the checkout, I became involved in an extraordinary exchange. It's all the more puzzling for being seemingly innocent and run-of-the-mill, but something about it unsettled me even then and it has continued to play on my mind to this day.

As I stood in line, I heard an unfamiliar voice say, "Hello," in a very familiar way. It was the greeting of someone whom one knows very well appearing in an unlikely situation or place. Something in the tone made me think that the "hello" was directed at me, and I turned expectantly, convinced that I was about to encounter a friend or neighbour, surprised to find me out of the normal confines of our village and instead queuing in the aisles of an out-of-town supermarket. My face must have registered confusion as I spun around to see, not a friend, but the woman from the café. She had greeted me as if she knew me very well and was standing looking at me as if she were expecting me to return her warm greeting in kind. My mind raced to place her. Did I know her from a toddler group? Was she friend of a friend? Was she a past client? No; I was certain that I had never clapped eyes on this exotically dressed redhead before seeing her in the café up the road just an hour beforehand. Perhaps this was how she greeted all strangers whose baby she had stopped to admire. I felt the uneasy feeling that sometimes occurs when a stranger, however pleasant, is slightly too much in your personal space. I was also distracted by Romy's restlessness and eager to get her back to the car, and our home. I smiled thinly at the woman and made to turn back to the checkout.

She wasn't finished with our interaction. Touching me gently on the arm, she continued, "I noticed you with your baby in the café just now. She's very special."

"Oh, thank you," I replied, softening slightly at this genuine and well-meant compliment to my child, "that's really kind of you. Obviously I think so too!"

She fixed me with a very direct gaze. It was kind and warm, but almost overwhelmingly intense to the point that it felt inappropriate. "No," she stated. "She really is something special." There was a pause before she relaxed into a smile and added, "She's beautiful."

I thanked her hastily, finished paying for our water and exited as fast as I could. I recall thinking something like, "What a fruitcake!" to myself as I hurried off. I didn't give her another thought until several days later, deep in grief. Without realising what I was saying, I started to tell Darius about the woman and before I could think I told him, "If we were in a film, this is the point where it would be revealed to the audience that the innocent stranger in the village café is actually an angel." I'm not entirely sure what Darius thought about my outburst but he had the good grace to roll with it and not to accuse me of having completely lost my mind.

There are in existence many films, newspaper articles and books detailing "angelic visitations" and I started to seek them out, to try to find some validity for what I was becoming increasingly convinced had been some kind of spiritual encounter. The best descriptions are those in which a complete stranger appears out of nowhere at the scene of an accident or similarly traumatic incident, offers help and then disappears. Sometimes these strangers are described as chameleons in the scene: the homeless man, the frail elderly lady, the nondescript-looking emergency room doctor. Others have told of striking and enigmatic characters who are impossible to ignore: the tall woman with long white hair who appears almost to glow; the dark-skinned man with a brooding countenance and lustrous hair, dressed in a suit when everyone else is casual. They all have one or two things in common, however: they are almost always described as "intense" in some way; their words or actions are always kind, compassionate or wise but can also be almost inappropriately abrupt. They appear apparently out of nowhere and disappear just as quickly, and an encounter with one of these beings stays with you and cannot be shaken. I have to say that I have never been able to revisit that café since I visited it with Romy. For a long time, though, I fantasised about returning a day or two later and asking the owner who the exotic-looking redhead was who had chatted so familiarly with her a few days before. I feel sure that I would have been told that the café owner did not know who, or what, I was talking about.

So: grief-stricken fantasy? Overactive imagination? Of course, it could be either of these or a mixture of both. I have lost count of the number of times I've replayed that exchange in my mind and each time I do so I become more convinced that the redhead in the café was another piece of the puzzle; a harbinger of what was to come, a way of gently reminding me of the contract I made before I came to be here. Whichever way I recall her, that woman was very determined to tell me that there was something extra special about my child.

Believing this piece of information helped me a lot as I started to piece together the events around Romy's short time with us. Putting my faith in the idea that Romy, Darius and I all planned this situation to enhance our spiritual learning has gone a long way to processing my grief and aided in my understanding of some very big questions, such as, "Why are we here?" Some may say that this requires a significant suspension of disbelief but, like so many other spiritual encounters and experiences in my life, this situation has emblazoned itself on my memory and whenever this happens I have come to understand that it is something I need to pay attention to. Of course, I will never know whether or not this woman was real, a product of my imagination, some kind of celestial being or simply an innocent passer-by I met in a café. For what it's worth, I believe that that woman was placed in that café at that time for a very specific reason. When I think of those two days in July 2014 I see all the people I encountered as players on a stage. I feel that on some subconscious level I was reconnecting with the plans I made with Romy's and Darius's souls before we came to be here, and that some of these interactions were planned to act as triggers, to remind me that somewhere deep in my soul, I chose this. I know that this may be very hard to believe, especially if your spiritual beliefs are not sympathetic with mine, but I can only speak my truth here.

During my time studying Spiritualism I have read many books about the afterlife, heaven, the spirit world – this place from whence we come and to which we return seems to have a plethora of acceptable names. I have seen this place, in my dreams and during meditations, which we use to open up to Spirit before doing mediumship but for many years I thought the images I saw were a very beautiful and ornate figment of my imagination. Then I began to read books by other mediums and to my amazement one or two of them described "my" version of the spirit world in the exact same detail. It looks and feels very real to me and over the years I have visited it in my mind many times.

In my version of this world, I have often seen a collective of light beings gathered inside a brilliant white cathedral-like building. Outside the building is a world filled with such vibrancy and colour that it almost hurts the eyes to look at it. Even to think of it lifts my spirits. In this world, no speech is necessary as all thoughts are pure and therefore able to be heard freely by all. If we wish to communicate to others, we simply direct our thoughts and they are heard and felt. The grass is verdant, the sky crystal clear and punctuated by the tips of towering brilliant white structures of such architectural beauty that the seven wonders of the world look pedestrian in comparison. Inside one of these buildings there are vast halls lined with shelf upon shelf of every book of learning imaginable. Tables are positioned at floor level and around these tables sit soul groups, or light being collectives, all looking intently at shimmering blue squares which have the appearance of maps. The beings of light are not in human form; they are more akin to shimmering columns of light with a very slight hint at a human outline. They are white or blue in colour and appear to the eye as being in perpetual motion; constantly shifting and changing. I have no idea how many individual beings make up a whole soul group but in my visions around these tables there always seems to be a group of six, eight or ten. They have gathered together to discuss the life purpose of one particular being, who is plotting their lifetime on earth and deciding what it is they wish to learn in that incarnation.

As I've said, I have had a deep interest in the afterlife and spiritualism for most of my adult life but after Romy passed I experienced a new drive to study and read about it in more detail. I was desperate to know, or at least find a suggestion of, where my daughter's soul, or spirit, might be. I knew unequivocally that she had to continue to exist somewhere: even in the throes of my grief I couldn't bring myself to believe that there is nothing at all after this life.

I have had almost four years to process the "loss" of my daughter and, believe me, my mind has gone back and forth from the world of spirit to some very dark and despairing places indeed. Asking myself what we all chose to learn has always somehow managed to help me to find some peace of mind. I imagine our souls – myself, Romy and Darius – communing together around one of those tables inside the cathedral-like building in the spirit world, putting the plans together and agreeing how we would each play our part. It feels conceivable to me that Darius and I agreed to take on the role of Romy's parents, knowing that she would not be with us for very long and that her departure would tear our lives apart and cause us immeasurable pain. Why? Because we each chose to experience the learning that comes from traumatic loss and grief during this lifetime. And because we made a choice to help Romy in her learning. In supporting her in her return to Spirit we helped her along on her journey as we would have done any other soul in our soul group, and which others have undoubtedly done for us in this life and in lifetimes past.

To me, so many things point to the idea that this situation was pre-planned. My sudden announcement that I would not be continuing with what I felt was my life's work just a week before Romy passed. Blurting out to my best friend that I had known that this was going to happen. Telling Romy that I didn't know what I would do without her. Telling her that I was committed to my promise to work for Spirit just hours before she became ill; telling her that it was our last day together on our way out that morning: the list goes on·and on. I am certain that some could explain away these simple nuances with no problems whatsoever, but they nag at me and they tell me that I chose this scenario because there was something very important that I have committed to do in this life.

That's not to say that I wouldn't trade almost anything to have my daughter here with me, physically growing up and changing in front of me. Each time I see a little girl at the age that she should be now on earth I feel a stab of pain. As much as it feels like the fulfilment of my life's dreams to work as an author and a medium, I would gladly carry out a mundane existence if I could have my child here with me. But this is not what I chose. Importantly, it is not what she chose either. She chose Darius and I as parents for this incarnation. It strikes me as significant that we have both always been spiritually curious people and that although our personality types are very different, we share many similarities in how we see the world and how we have both always felt a little like outsiders. We have experienced many differences during our time together and have come to know that they come together in a productive way during times of challenge. I have always thought that this is because we share the very simple but powerful perspective that it is through difficulty that we learn the most. Rather than throw ourselves on the floor in desperation, we have faced up to each challenge and committed ourselves to extracting new knowledge from it.

You might be asking yourself how anything positive can possibly ever come from the death of a child but I would counter this by asking what would be achieved by seeing only the negative. Right from the earliest days Darius and I were determined that Romy's life should mean something to others as well as to us, but not just in the sense that we wanted her to be remembered. We saw the extent to which she had touched others during her short time here and we both felt that there was a deep reason for this. I felt that it was some kind of pointer for me to recommence my work with Spirit – something that I had promised to do if Romy came to be with me here. The later suggestion from more than one medium that Romy's purpose in the world of spirit was great made me think that the work that could be done by me here in her absence is also inspired by her. This book, which I hope very much may reach those who seek answers and comfort following the passing of a loved one to Spirit, would not exist if it weren't for Romy's passing.

Some have said that if it weren't for Romy's death then Macsen, our youngest son, would not exist either but this I cannot agree with. I always had a deep knowing that I would have four children. When we went to sign off with the hospital after Romy's birth (a requirement in the UK when you have had a home birth and subsequent visits from midwives), our midwife Lisa jokingly asked if she would be seeing us again. Darius replied very swiftly in the negative but I hesitated, which caused much hilarity. Even though I was forty-one-years old, had spent over a year beleaguering my husband for a third child and even though I had an apparently healthy baby in my arms, I heard myself say, "Well, if I weren't in my forties, maybe just one more..." I believe that all four of my children were meant to exist and it does sometimes feel cruel that I had no idea that one of them wouldn't stay to grow up with me, but when I look at things from a spiritual perspective, it makes sense.

One other "player on the stage" that day feels particularly significant. Just after Romy's birth we started to discuss moving away from the village and closer to Brighton, and we invited a couple of estate agents over to the house. Suddenly alarmed at the prospect of the evaluator arriving to our house full of nappies, empty coffee mugs and children's toys littering the floor I decided to hire a cleaner to give the whole house a once-over on the morning of 17th July.

As I arrived home with Romy around lunchtime that day, our cleaner was just finishing. She had done an amazing job and I quipped that I felt as if I had come home to the wrong house. I asked her if she'd like to join me for a cup of tea before she left and it was just after I went to put the kettle on that I heard the awful noise that took me a few moments to place but which turned out to be the sound of Romy's laboured breathing. As events unfolded like wildfire, I went into shock and froze, panic-stricken. Afterwards, I had the feeling that this woman had somehow been put in my home that day because she flew into action and was utterly amazing. It turned out that her main job was as an in-flight attendant and she was fully trained in first aid. As I virtually collapsed on my living room floor she went into autopilot and all her training kicked in. She flew about, checking Romy's breathing, putting her in the recovery position and taking the phone from me to speak to the 999 operator.

A few weeks later, I managed to get in contact with her as I felt strongly that I needed to see her in person to thank her for everything she had done that day. It was a very emotional meeting for us both and we agreed that we share a unique bond after having experienced such a traumatic event together. However, what I didn't expect was that during our meeting, she told me that she had also lost a daughter as a baby. We cried together and somehow I think that we understood that we were put in each other's path in order to help each other. It wasn't immediately apparent exactly how being present at this awful happening could help this lady but months later she told me that she had spent a great deal of time thinking over both our experiences and that it had in some small way helped her to process the loss of her own daughter. I still wonder whether or not she understands exactly how important her role was to me that day. I honestly do not know how things would have unfolded had she not been with me at such a crucial time of need.

Prompt: Have you ever encountered a person in life who seems to have been "put in your way" in a very deliberate move? This could be someone who has helped or hindered you. Has someone's actions diverted you from an accident or major life decision that you may have regretted? Are there any particular situations that are "freeze-framed" in your mind? Do you need to "unfreeze" them?

Chapter 8

Through The Door

Death is the continuing of life... the next part of our life. It's like walking through a door, you know? Walking through the door marked "Death": it's the beginning of a new part of our journey.
– **Rosemary Altea**

Never in the time since my daughter's passing have I spoken, or even written, in full about exactly what happened in that room in King's College Hospital at around 4pm on Friday 18th July 2014. I say "around 4pm" because, much to our surprise, we ended up alone in that room with Romy as she passed to Spirit and were so wrapped up in events that we did not think to look at a clock and no one was in attendance to announce the time of her passing.

After we had made the agonising decision to switch off all the life support paraphernalia the hospital staff swung into action, preparing things quietly, respectfully and efficiently while we sat shell-shocked in an anteroom, waiting for the inevitable. Darius began calling family members to tell them what was happening and I remember hearing the phrase, "We're just waiting for them to start turning everything off," over and over again. Each time I heard it, I became aware of a primal howling sound, which I realised was coming from me. After three or four calls I was on my knees on the floor, howling. The calls stopped. I couldn't find a voice to call even my parents or my sister so I sent a text message to Claire, my sister who had left us just a few hours before, passing on the terrible information, apologising for the way I was delivering it and asking if she could please tell Mum and Dad for us.

Eventually the registrar came in and started to talk about what would happen. Ever since we had arrived at King's she had been mispronouncing Romy's name, saying "Rommie" as opposed to "Ro-mee". Suddenly this was unbearable. "I'm sorry," I snapped at her, "but could you at least pronounce her name properly if you're telling us she's going to die?" The poor woman apologised profusely with the air of somebody who has had many such exchanges with parents who are about to say goodbye to a child. She understood that this was less about her mispronunciation of our daughter's name and everything to do with me trying desperately to prevent the words I was dreading from coming out of her mouth. She resumed talking.

I stopped her mid-flow a second time as I realised that she was referring to an event that would be taking place in the PICU. "Wait a minute," I said, "we're not going to be out there are we?" Anxious looks shot between the staff members which was enough to tell me that yes, they were going to draw the curtain around Romy's bed, switch everything off and we were going to sit with her until she passed. In the middle of PICU, surrounded by very sick children and their hollow-eyed, desperate parents. My first thought was, "I'm going to lose it – let out all the emotion, howl, scream, shout – how can I do this in front of these poor people who are sitting with their sick children and witnessing their pain and suffering? What is it going to do to them to see us going through this with our child?" This was swiftly followed by the thought, "I am not going to let my daughter die in that ward, in public. It is not going to be like this." I asked as politely as I could whether it might be possible for us to be in the side room that the staff had so kindly made available for Darius and I and Claire to rest in. They immediately agreed and set about making it ready for us. My relief was palpable.

I'm not sure why but I assumed that, due to some kind of health and safety reasons, we would not be permitted to be alone in the room with Romy. I thought that there would be a doctor or nurse sitting discreetly in a corner. Let's face it, I had been asked so many times to go over and over the events of the previous morning that I had got the clear impression that certain protocols were in place. They felt unsavoury but I was so deep in shock that I barely registered the intrusive questioning and understood that it was necessary that these processes existed. Darius did notice and he confessed that seeing me being repeatedly asked, in a thinly veiled way, whether I had harmed my own child pushed him pretty close to his limit.

Up until now, the events that followed on that day have seemed almost a sacred event to be shared only by Darius and myself. Only he and I know exactly what transpired in that room and although we have our own personal recollections and memories, it is a unique situation that bonds us together, much like the birth of a child. However, now, in the spirit of the truth that we associate so strongly with Romy, sharing my recollection of the passing of my precious daughter feels like a gift to pass on. As I begin to write the words I feel a little reluctant, as if this letting go is going to leave me feeling bereft yet again, but I know that sharing it is the right thing to do. I knew at the time that it was imperative for me to be able to speak of Romy's passing as a way of helping others and for the opportunity for those others, and for me, to heal. In fact, I whispered a promise to her that I would write it all down.

We have been fortunate to birth all four of our children at home, attended by a minimal number of professionals who have respected our space, wishes and surroundings (excepting the case of our older daughter Layla, whose arrival was so fast that we welcomed her on our own, with a nineteen-month-old Kasper in attendance). Having worked for many years as a birth doula, attending numerous births in all kinds of environments, it is my view that witnessing the arrival of a new life into the world carries immense privilege. I also believe that helping a soul to pass is the same. I feel honoured to have been able to sit with my daughter and help her to pass to the next stage of her journey and I know that, had I not had that opportunity, it would have haunted me. I believe that Spirit enabled me to experience this to aid me in my healing and also to help with the healing of others.

Still, I am human and I have had to steel myself to write these words because for all my spiritual beliefs I am afraid. Afraid of reliving the experience yet again. Afraid that sending such a precious memory and intimate beliefs out into the world may result in my being ridiculed or considered crazy in some way. Afraid, once again, of letting go.

So, back to that room, to which I am physically and emotionally unable to return and yet which I have visited so often in my mind. We returned to King's two days after Romy passed as they couldn't release her to us until certain paperwork was complete. Not thinking straight, not knowing where to go and acting on autopilot, we found our way up to PICU, and as soon as we got within a few steps of the unit, my legs collapsed and I couldn't breathe. Although the association I have with that room is an obviously negative one, I can say without hesitation that what happened in it was truly beautiful. My memories of those 48 hours of 17th and 18th July 2014 are patchy at best due to the state of deep shock I was in but my recollection of that final hour with my daughter on this earth is crystal clear.

Somewhere around 3pm they wheeled Romy's bed into the room where Darius and I were waiting. There were several staff members, including a senior doctor we had spoken to at length over the 24 hours we had been at King's, and the PICU nurse on duty at that time, Kat. If earth angels really do exist, Kat is one such being. She instinctively knew exactly how to behave with us: volunteering information, asking questions about our preferences and speaking easily about Romy as a real, living person present in the room, without awkwardness. This is no easy task to perform with two parents desperate with grief.

The doctor explained that her colleagues were beginning the process of unhooking and removing all the extraneous equipment and machines with their bleeps and wires, and that the final thing to be removed would be the oxygen tube. While they were detaching all the equipment I approached the bed to hold Romy's hand and realised I was standing next to the doctor. In a surreal and touching moment, she put her arm around me and I realised that she was crying. I registered the ludicrous thought, "She's not supposed to cry – it's not professional. Is she allowed to do that?" but I was comforted to see that a senior medical professional was not afraid to show her emotion. It helped to know that she cared so much.

Kat explained gently that once Romy's oxygen supply was removed then she would no longer be able to breathe unaided and although she would not be in any discomfort as her system was still full of morphine, it may take a while before she actually chose to leave. I had to stop myself from telling her that no, it would be very quick. Aside from feeling that she had already "gone" in many senses on our living room sofa the day before, I also knew without a shadow of a doubt that Romy had completed whatever it was she had come here to do and that, just as she had been conceived and born quickly, she would leave in just such a determinedly focussed way.

Darius and I sat on the bed and Kat gently picked Romy up and brought her over to place in my arms, still with her breathing tube in. They removed it carefully and I recall my relief when they took off the sticking plaster that had taped it to her mouth. It had been disturbing me that she had this obstruction to her mouth – mother's instinct at work.

I glanced at Darius, sitting to my right on the bed. He was utterly broken and just couldn't keep it together. My emotionally controlled husband, who I knew better than anyone and whom I had never seen cry in over a decade together, was sobbing in pain and I found it almost unbearable to witness. I realised that he was trying to position himself so that he could touch Romy and feel that he was also holding her in some way and I knew that his protective father's instinct was prompting him to somehow help her to feel safe. He asked me to shift along slightly on the bed so he could place his hands underneath her and hold her with me. I didn't need to think about my words, they were out of my mouth before I realised I'd had the thought. "You hold her," I said to him. He looked at me for a moment in bewilderment. "No, no, you hold her, I wasn't asking you to pass her to me. I'm sorry."

It was so clear to me. In fact, at that moment everything was completely calm, lucid and clear. I had spent a lot of the past 24 hours in a maelstrom of howling, crying, in a state of near collapse and in shocked numbness but in that room, at that time, I felt an extraordinary sense of calm and knowing descend on me. "I can fall apart afterwards," I recall thinking. "Right now, Romy needs me. I need to be here for her and I need to help her to do this." To Darius, I heard myself say, "No, she came into your hands and she should go out from them. I carried her inside me for nine months and I spent every minute of every day of her life together with her. You were the first person to touch her and it's absolutely right that you should be the last."

I passed her across to him as if she were made of glass. Darius, still sitting to my right, held her with her head pointing to the right and her feet towards my lap. We both kissed her and I put the index finger of my right hand gently inside her curled left hand, still so small.

And so we sat. The energy in the room was indescribably still and light, much like the atmosphere at a birth. Having spent the best part of a decade accompanying birthing women I recognised this energy immediately. It's a little like a much-visited place of worship or a sacred site. There is a reverence, a deep stillness and a sense of being frozen in time. There is a very fine line between immense privilege and feeling like an intruder. At some point I looked up to see where the nurse or medical professional had stationed themselves, but to my shock there was nobody there. I don't know how it happened but the only people in that room were me, Darius and Romy; and then numerous spirit people whose presence and light began to fill up the room.

For a moment, it's as if time stood still and then zeroed in on our small triad and nothing existed outside it. Darius was still crying quietly but within a few moments I became very aware of a second shift in the room's energy. This may sound strange but it suddenly felt like a party atmosphere. Yes, this took me completely by surprise as well. Never in my life did I imagine writing a sentence suggesting that at the moment of my child's passing there was a party-like atmosphere in the room, but this is what it was.

The room began to fill up with an intense, electrifying energy and I felt myself immediately uplifted. It felt joyous and I experienced a heightened sense of excitement and anticipation. I could see, in my mind's eye – the part of my mind I see as being like a cinema screen when I'm doing sittings – a vibrant golden light which seemed to have come from nowhere and was filling up the whole room. The sense of celebration and joy was so overwhelming I began to feel excited. "The energy's changing, there are people here to meet her, can you feel it? Can you feel it?" I asked Darius with urgent excitement, but he said that he couldn't. I began to sense the presence of people in spirit, both those I have known and those I haven't: my grandparents, Darius's aunt Jeannette who had passed just nine days before, his father, Noory, whom I had never met. There was a sense of gathering, of a crowd of familiar people coming together. It felt friendly, warm and, yes, celebratory. They were coming to meet Romy, to gather her up and take her with them, to celebrate the lesson she had completed during her brief time here on earth.

I looked at Romy and could see her whole face changing before my eyes, as if the pallor of the past two days was lifting and she was drinking in the golden light. The room was suffused in it. I heard words from somewhere and realised that it was my own voice talking to her. My index finger was still tucked within the fingers of her left hand. "Romy," I said, "they're all here for you. It's okay, you can go with them." I held my breath, perhaps expecting to hear a disembodied voice or some angelic music, but there was only the sound of Darius's quiet sobs in the stillness of the room.

"Mummy and Daddy love you so much, Romy, but it's time to go now. You need to go towards the light. Can you see the light, darling? It's safe and they're all there waiting for you. We love you so much. We're going to hold your hand until you get to them."

And then, the signal I had been waiting for. Romy's left hand squeezed my finger with a strength I would not have thought possible. She took a deep breath in and let out a small sigh. I felt the energy lifting still further, it was spiralling into a frenzy. "She's going, can you feel it? It's incredible!" I almost shouted at Darius. He looked at me but I could not register what he was witnessing.

For me, the whole room had disappeared and the three of us were suspended in a vortex of golden light, surrounded by angelic beings and those we loved in spirit. It was the most amazing experience of my life.

And then, it was gone. Where we had been holding our daughter, we were all of a sudden holding her body, an empty shell. It was so obviously not Romy, it had even stopped looking like her a little bit because the essence of her had just left. I've never taken drugs but I imagine that the feeling I began to experience at that point was something like what they call "coming down". I descended fast, reality slapping my face on the way down to signal that my life had just changed irrevocably. My daughter, my precious, longed for third child, was no longer with us. The howling began again: the deep, guttural, primal outpouring that felt as if it were coming from somewhere outside my body. I lost all sense of time, place and surroundings. I heard my voice screaming, "My baby! My baby!" and my body folded in on itself. The intensity of the physical pain was breathtaking. I felt like a wild animal in pain and I would have done anything to make it stop. At this point, Darius and I perceptibly swapped positions. I ceased being the calm, clear one and quite literally fell to the floor, broken. He stopped sobbing, visibly straightened up and became as solid as a rock. He would continue like this, steadfastly holding me up over the months and years to come.

We sat with Romy for over an hour in that room. Once the hysteria subsided a little, Kat appeared like a magic angel and started to gently ask us about clothing, washing and whether or not we would like a lock of hair (we did). Someone came in to ask if we would like to have casts made of Romy's hands and feet. Despite the fact that I had asked my friend Natasha to help me to make a belly cast while I was pregnant, for some reason I found the idea of casting her little hands and feet disturbing. I also felt very strongly about photographs – I did not want any. I knew from my work as a doula that many couples find photographs of their child or children immensely comforting when there has been a stillbirth and again I was surprised at my refusal, but I was emphatic about this point and I have not regretted it.

I stand by my stance on photographs as now, three years on, I still struggle with mental images of her body and they spring up and haunt me in the most unlikely situations. I can imagine that if a child has been stillborn and his or her parents have not had an opportunity to see them living, breathing, smiling and laughing then photographs must be an immense comfort. I was fortunate enough to have memories of Romy living and it unsettles me to encounter imagery of her body once her spirit had passed, although I must stress that this is not a judgement on others' decisions. I recall a conversation I had with Natasha, who is a talented photographer and took beautiful photographs of Romy at ten days old, which are among my most treasured possessions. A week or two before Romy was born we sat in a local café chatting about the belly cast and Natasha's new venture into newborn photography. I told her that, as a doula, I saw a clear and emerging need for photographers with a little extra something to offer their services to parents who endure the agony of stillbirth. I suggested to her that she could consider this alongside her newborn photography. As it turned out, it wasn't a direction she felt comfortable going in but I find it strange that we had that conversation at that time. The belly cast is boxed in our basement and I am resigned to a lifetime of not knowing what to do with it. My dreams of painting it in vibrant colours and displaying it somewhere (discreet) in our home have vanished. I also cannot bear to part with it, so closely is it tied with that pregnancy and all its associated feelings of excitement and joy. I have often thought it strange that I never chose to make a belly cast in any of my other pregnancies – only Romy's.

One of the most common phrases any of us who have lost a loved one, let alone a child, in a sudden or traumatic way will hear is, "I can't imagine what you have been through." I include this description of Romy's passing to Spirit, not because I wish to upset anyone, or to spell out the agony of "losing" a child. I include it because, even at the time that it happened, it was not the worst part of the experience. The moment of Romy's passing, for me, was one of the most otherworldly, privileged and uplifting experiences I have ever had. On a human level, as a parent, letting go of my child in this way was as unimaginably awful as you might imagine it to be, if not worse. However, I would still say that the days, weeks, months and years after that moment were harder than the moment itself.

Death is not the end. It is not a negative experience, it is a return home. We hear and see these sentiments everywhere and they probably resonate with many; until, that is, they experience the passing of one of their own. Then the words become trite and empty as we believe that nobody could possibly imagine the agony that we are going through without our loved one. These feelings were very real for me, but the reason I believe that I can sit here years later writing these words is because I believe absolutely in what I write. Because I have the ability to be able to open up to Spirit, and because that opportunity was afforded to me during my child's passing I am able to tell others that her return home to our soul group was a cause for celebration in the spirit world, and for just a few seconds I was allowed to witness and be part of that celebration.

If you think about it, it's exactly what you would do for your child, or any loved one. Imagine if your child arrived home one day and announced that they had decided to apply for a university place to study as a doctor because they wanted to heal and help as many people as possible. Most of us would be impressed by our offspring's dedication and level of commitment, not to mention compassion for others. We would feel as if we had done our job well. As a loving, responsible parent we would of course discuss and plan this with our child and do as much as we could to help them achieve their dream, their purpose. Now imagine that your child then said, "Mum/Dad listen, I want to be the most incredible doctor in the world and I know how I can do this but it's going to mean asking something of you." Most of us would agree without question but imagine that we had the power to somehow elevate our child to a position in which they could heal, or help, many, many people. Imagine if this involved saying goodbye to our child for many years as they went away to study intensively. If we knew that the end result would be something as huge, for example, as a cure for cancer or the establishment of world peace, would we agree?

This is similar to what I have come to feel about Romy's passing. I can't pretend to know what her purpose was, or what it was she came here to learn. Jan suggested that she needed to come here for a brief time to learn unconditional love –

something she received abundantly in her short time on earth. During a sitting with my dear friend Gerrie March in November 2014, she suggested that Romy's purpose now she has returned to Spirit is to aid in the resolution of world conflict. Interestingly, Gerrie talked at some length during that sitting about how unpredictable various world situations would become and also said that many artists and creative people would be "going home" as she put it, over the course of the year to come. Since then, we are witnessing increasingly erratic behaviour from our world leaders, and 2016 was a year in which a seemingly unprecedented number of world famous or iconic artists passed. Gerrie might have been a year too early but she was certainly accurate.

I believe that Romy is a highly evolved soul and only required a short time here on earth to complete her learning before returning to Spirit. Several mediums I have consulted all offered that she would not be returning – by which they meant reincarnating in some way – and I knew this for myself. As soon as I began to entertain the idea of having another baby I asked myself whether this was because I thought that Romy might somehow return to me. Walter Makichen's book lists several case studies in which something similar has happened. However, I knew in my heart that I would not be meeting her again in this lifetime and I accepted that. I also had a strong feeling that, once she had communicated to me that she had returned safely and that her passing had not been traumatic for her, I would not have contact again for some time. So far, this has held true.

For anyone who might be dismissing these words as the ramblings of a grief-stricken mother, I can't argue with you, any more than I can argue against a Christian who believes that their loved ones go to heaven to be with God or those who believe that once we take our last breath the curtain falls for all eternity. However, I know that if I had to choose between there being nothing after this life and there being an afterlife in which I would meet my loved ones again I know that I would choose what I believe now. It might not be true. I believe that I have evidence, as far as you can call it that, to suggest that it is, but this is only based on my personal experiences, some of which have been corroborated independently by mediums who did not previously know me or my situation at all, and one that did. And of course, I respect the fact that to the scientific world nothing I can describe would legitimately count as evidence, or proof, of anything.

There is always an argument. Perhaps these mediums might have "read" me. Perhaps I am vulnerable, gullible. Having spent years training in psychic development and mediumship myself I'm pretty certain that I'd know if I was being taken for a ride, but I am open to all opinions, comments and suggestions. It always comes back to the same thing: I cannot for the life of me see any harm in believing what I do as it paints a positive picture of the process that we call dying. If we choose to see this as a transition, a journey from one world to the next, just like birth, then I think that life becomes altogether more colourful and full of hope. This is the way that I prefer to live my life, and believe me, that has been a struggle sometimes as I have coped with the symptoms of depression and Post Traumatic Stress Disorder without ever having taken a single dose of medication.

Being present for the transition of my daughter was just as big a privilege, in my opinion, as being able to bring her forth into this world to breathe life. Just as I had imagined I would, I fell apart in the days after she passed, when the realisation that I could no longer hold, care for or protect my child began to dawn on me. The human level of possessiveness strengthened by the intense responsibility of parenthood kicked in, and from this perspective I just couldn't see how I could carry on with my life without my baby. I would have done anything to physically hold on to her, but all I could do was desperately try to keep alive the memory of her leaving as it was so full of hope, life and light. It was to take me a while longer than I had hoped before that memory transcended the pain of my grief.

Prompt: If someone close to you has died, where do you think they are now? Lying in the ground? In the spirit world, afterlife, or heaven? Do you speak to them or feel their presence around you? How do you think they feel? Have you ever been privileged to accompany someone in their final moments on earth? What was the energy like? How did it feel, for you and for them?

Chapter 9

After

To heal the wound, you need to go into the dark night of the soul.
– Tori Amos

Parts of the immediate aftermath of Romy's passing are still, almost four years later, difficult for me to recall. My father has a theory that this, and my ongoing PTSD related memory loss, is a result of my brain immediately "shutting down" in July 2014 in an attempt to protect me from the trauma that I was experiencing. So adept has my mind become at blocking out the events of those days that it is still physically difficult to retrieve them. What's more, this technique has proved so successful that my brain is also skilled at erasing all sorts of other important day-to-day information. Regardless of whether or not I write notes in my diary, on a chalkboard in my kitchen or scrawl it in marker pen on my hand, my brain struggles to retrieve information of a practical nature.

Up until July 2014 I thought I had seen my fair share of dramas. Nothing in comparison to some, but I had experienced some difficult times emotionally and prided myself on being a strong person; someone who could navigate her way through a challenging life situation and, with the help of a positive outlook, come out the other side reasonably intact. I have never believed in holding grudges, will always try to see the good in people even if they have let me down and try my best (although I have not always succeeded) to leave the past behind and keep moving forwards.

Having studied literature I was familiar with the term "dark night of the soul" and after Romy died the phrase kept getting into my head. Grief seemed to me to be all encompassing. On a mental and emotional level, it really did feel as if I were sliding into a dark vortex from which there was no return and I found that there was a very real physical feeling attached to my grief. My heart physically hurt and my body had strange aches and pains. I had a constant sense of sliding downwards, accompanied by a nagging feeling of having forgotten something. I might lose myself for a minute; smile, laugh or engage with the children and then it would hit me: a feeling of restlessness, of something being left behind. Then I would remember: my daughter was dead. The initial cataclysmic feelings of desperation and horror gradually began to give way to a subtly creeping realisation that every parent's worst nightmare was, in fact, my new reality. I was being sucked into a void of hopelessness and it was a daily struggle to keep myself from going under.

Having been refused some by my GP on the grounds that it was "too soon" and that it was better to receive counselling, "... in around three months' time, when it will get really bad" (yes, she really did utter those words), I asked my wonderful sister-in-law Nuria to help and she spent several hours calling round various organisations. It was through this kindness that we were set up with counselling visits from Cruse Bereavement and regular phone calls with a woman called Sue at Child Bereavement UK. As time passed I found that I entered a state of "counselling overload" and its benefits began to dwindle but on these early days it gave us the platform we so needed to talk through our grief with a neutral person who listened, made practical suggestions and helped us to inch forward one small step at a time. Other than this, when it came to professional support we were largely on our own and things were about to get more challenging.

For three years or so leading up to Romy's birth Darius had been in a business partnership with two other men. Together, the three of them possessed complementary skills that they felt provided excellent service delivering graduate recruitment and leadership development programmes. However, after a decade running businesses in this environment Darius had developed some innovative ideas. To me, he was ready to strike out on his own.

Towards the end of my pregnancy with Romy I had begun to have a feeling that all was not well with Darius's work. Not wanting to worry me when I was about to give birth, he reassured me that things were fine. When we eventually talked through the situation I found myself telling him to get out and go it alone. "You're ready," I told him. "You have exactly the right blend of skills and experience to go out there on your own. Why don't you talk to the others, tell them you want out and find a good way for you to all exit amicably and move on?" Darius resisted taking this route as he was considering his partners, neither of whom he thought felt as ready as he did to strike out independently. He was adamant that he would work through a solution for the business that served them all.

After Romy died we faced an unstable situation as a family. Darius, who is self-employed and was at that time the sole earner, took a couple of months off on compassionate leave, which were of course unpaid. During this time his two partners decided that they no longer wanted to continue with the partnership and it came to an abrupt and not entirely amicable end. Although Darius emerged from this period with a new clarity about exactly what it was he wanted to do, negotiating a harmonious resolution to this business "divorce" became an emotionally draining experience for us both. Coming as it did just after we had lost Romy, it felt like an enormous blow. On top of all the stress I felt dismay that alongside having to process our daughter's death we were now seemingly being thrown another impossible situation by The Universe. How much worse could it get? What was next?

For us, this served as a stark reminder that sometimes, even when we think that things can't get any worse, life deals us another blow. We might find it impossible to understand. We might rail against it. We might pity ourselves. More than once I found myself wailing at Darius, "What on earth have we done to deserve all this?" The key is absolutely how we choose to act in such situations, and how it lends light to our understanding of the path we have chosen. Even though I considered the break-up of the partnership to be a good thing, the way in which it happened was immensely upsetting and it was a real challenge to find our way through it all when our energy was already so depleted.

It took me a long time before I returned to the words of Jan, the medium and friend of Michelle's whom we had seen at her home in Kent just after Romy passed. In that email she had sent before even meeting us Jan had said, "It is some people's mission to go into a darkness in order to find the light. You can't always see the light in the light, but you can see it in the darkness." At the time, this made no sense to me whatsoever. I assumed that she was referring to the grief of losing a child; I couldn't imagine any experience darker than this. However, when I reread her words, I was struck by how they appeared to hint at an additional sense of darkness and I now believe that this refers to the experience we had with the ending of Darius's business.

Rather than fight, fall into despair or withdraw from one another, we sat down each evening and we talked. We talked about Romy, we talked about why, we talked about the end of the business partnership. We asked what it was we were missing. We made a firm decision to respond to any negativity and unpleasantness with grace and love, as much as we could. I know that to some this might appear weak or ineffective, but I can tell you that for us, it worked like a miracle. For every difficult turn the situation took we rallied and tried to send love; to each other and to everyone involved. Time and again we would return to asking ourselves, "What are we supposed to learn?" "Why did we choose to put this in our path?"

The answers we came up with were several. My theory was that Darius was always meant to be working alone: however, he has a deep-seated sense of duty to others and an innate kindness which I believe means that he would never have taken the step away from that partnership – so clearly wrong for him – without a catalyst. He did go on to work solo, as I had suggested he might, and today he enjoys a successful career that blends his own particular brand of leadership coaching with working with a large international company specialising in neuroscience. He couldn't have written a better career path for himself, and yet if that partnership had not ended in that way at that time it's unlikely that he would be enjoying the success and happiness he is today.

It took longer for me to come up with a theory as to how the situation would serve me. I spent so long entrenched in my outrage and anger that I couldn't see past my emotions. After a while I began to wonder whether it wasn't a useful lesson from Spirit. When you lose a child, you become a number of different things to different people and their ways of coping with your loss are many and varied. To some, you are a social pariah. They cross the street or zoom down another supermarket aisle when they see you, they don't invite you to gatherings or parties and if they do find themselves in conversation with you they can't help but tell you about their own losses or begin filling you in with gossip from the school gates. To others, you take on some kind of saintly status; you can absolutely do no wrong. If I had taken a sledgehammer to an innocent person's car and smashed their windscreen with no explanation, the whispered response would still have been, "Poor thing, she lost her child." Still others become afraid of talking to you about their losses or tragedies. One friend endured the terror of cancer not long after Romy passed and bless her, whenever we spoke about her progress, she would immediately follow everything she said with, "Of course, this is nothing compared to what you're going through." This is well meaning, but it is incorrect. We all have our challenges to face and none is "worse" than the other.

While searching online for support groups I came across a term that made me laugh out loud: "Grief Olympics". This is a term applied to those who have become so caught up in their grief that they feel the need to outdo each other with how bad they are feeling. If this sounds uncharitable, it is; but there is also a grain of truth in it. For me, in the early days, these virtual groups offered fantastic support in the form of a safe community where I could express my feelings that others around me couldn't possibly understand but I quickly stepped away from them. The reason? I felt that some of these people were still entrenched in their grief. Whether we like it or not, life continues. It continues without our loved ones and it will continue without us. Insisting that everyone honour our loved ones in Spirit by referring to them in every conversation and remembering each and every birthday and anniversary is not only exhausting for us and for them, but it serves no purpose and distracts us from our life. I am not suggesting that we airbrush our deceased loved ones from our lives, but that we start to see the positivity in remembering them in our own small, personal ways. For example, I buy Romy a bouquet of fresh roses each week and place them on my desk next to her photograph, talking to her as I arrange them. This helps me to feel my connection to her and brings her presence quietly into our family space without forcing it.

As much as it pained me to put one foot in front of the other, I pushed myself to do this. I sought out the Spiritualist church because I wanted to move forwards. For many bereaved parents it becomes important to seek answers or, perhaps, an organisation or individual on whom to place blame. In cases where there has clearly been negligence, I can completely understand this need but I also saw it in others who had no cause to pursue it. Personally, we had nothing but admiration, gratitude and respect for the many medical professionals who helped us and from the earliest days of our grief we both recognised that seeking answers can fast turn into a slippery slope. In some cases, I believe that it can also hold us back in our grieving process as we can become stuck in the past, unable to release our loved one as we are still looking for someone to hold accountable for their absence in our lives.

Romy's passing made us both question the very root of our beings. It challenged our spiritual beliefs, our relationship and the entire family life we had built in the most intense way. We could have crumbled. We could have bent our heads, become people who were spoken about as "never being the same again" after our loss, or we could rise up and honour our daughter and our chosen purposes by shining the light for others. The aftermath of Romy's passing was a time of great nurturing and care and I sometimes wonder whether, had the situation with Darius's business not occurred, we might still be lingering in that collective hug. When your energy is sapped (exactly as Jan had said it was) it becomes all too easy to keep doing whatever you were doing before, to sit tight and not to take risks or strike out into a new unknown. Perhaps Darius and I needed an extra push to show us the way into our new life. The discomfort of our situation meant that we strove to move forwards and within six months we had sold our house, moved to a new area, moved the children's school and learned that we were expecting a new baby. Darius had begun to lay foundations for his new business, and while I was in a sense frozen with regard to my work, I was spending valuable time rediscovering my connection to Spiritualism in preparation for my new purpose, just as I had promised Romy. The collapse of the business shook us out of our safe haven and forced us to take a long hard look at every aspect of our lives. It made us stand up and fight for our beliefs, and it made us see the truth of what those beliefs were. Having spent most of my life hiding my mediumistic abilities I began to gravitate once again to those who could help me develop them.

The whole of those first six months we saw time and again how Romy had brought truth to our lives in such significant ways. We began to see that it was no coincidence that we gave to her the name Satya.

In case you have somehow emerged from reading this chapter with the idea that life was so spiritually wonderful after Romy's death that we didn't experience any of the grief that "normal" people do, I'll balance it out now. Emotions were raw, very raw. I became paranoid about the children's health and when, days after the funeral, Layla careered into the conservatory, slipped and banged her head on the side of a chair, drawing blood, I became hysterical, screaming and panicking so much I almost hyperventilated. It was our five-year-old son who had to help Darius find a first aid kit and clean up what was essentially a small graze. On the way home from dropping the children at school I would fantasise about how fast I needed to drive into a roadside tree in order to kill myself. I would look at people pushing girl babies in prams and feel a deep-seated hatred for them that shocked me to my core. I wished their baby were dead instead of mine. I had dropped spectacularly into an abyss and what was worrying was how adept I became at pretending to the outside world that I was coping. I wasn't.

Remarkably, Darius and I only had one major argument in the whole of those first few months and naturally it was over something as surreal and ridiculous as the seating plan for our child's funeral. I can't recall the detail but it culminated in my screaming at Darius, running through the house like a madwoman and hurling a drink at my laptop as it sat innocently on the kitchen worktop. I continued my rampage into the garden and flung myself down on the lawn next to the rose bush we had planted for Romy, desperately wishing that the ground would swallow me up. After several moments of sobbing I was hit with the dawning realisation that my laptop had on it photographs of the children – of Romy. I froze for a moment before running screeching back into the house and yelling incoherently at Darius that we had to take the laptop to a repair shop *now*. I drove like a maniac into town, scraping the side of the car badly as I careered into the underground car park and raced into the computer store. Goodness knows what they must have thought when I arrived, dishevelled and garbling about irreplaceable photos of my dead daughter that must be retrieved. I am usually highly impressed with their customer service but am sad to say that on this occasion they continued to calmly repeat that I would need to book an appointment and that there was a three-day wait. It was all too much and I left in floods of tears. I thank my lucky stars for my dear friend Em, at that time my near neighbour, who received my frantic text message and quietly arrived to take the laptop away to someone she knew could recover the photographs, which I couldn't even bear to look at. My parents accompanied me into town to help me to buy a new laptop, which I couldn't afford. I am sitting typing on that very thing now, and bless my parents they never did accept my offer to repay them for it.

As the days after Romy's passing rolled into weeks, I remained cocooned in my bubble of shock. Being in shock is actually a healing process; it prevents you from feeling, thinking or emoting; you simply exist to function. The feeling is akin to being in a type of fog. My days were still taken up with caring for our two older children through the remainder of the long summer holiday, and by the time they returned to school we had put our house on the market so any time I might have spent feeling lonely and depressed was employed clearing the house and speaking to estate agents. When I wasn't doing that I was running the house, cooking, cleaning, shopping and doing everything I could to avoid facing up to my grief. I did all of this on some kind of autopilot.

Days after Romy's death my brain, desperately seeking a way out of my emotional and mental torment, had begun to entertain thoughts of suicide. I didn't realise at that time that this is a typical reaction to grief: it can feel so overpowering, so immense, that your primal instinct is to run, but of course, who can run from their own mind? At particularly bleak and desperate times, removing yourself from the situation can seem like the only viable option. While a part of me couldn't imagine actually going through with anything, the thoughts were terrifying, and frequent. Eventually I went and spoke with my neighbour, a previously active man who had become paralysed in an accident some years before and who remained a wheelchair user. A kind man and a good listener, our children loved him and spent many happy hours running in and out of his house and garden. "Tell me," I asked one particularly awful day as I sat at his kitchen table, "you must have had times when you wanted to kill yourself. How did you stop yourself from actually going through with it?"

"Ah yes," he replied, "of course, I planned it in meticulous detail so many times."

"So, what stopped you?"

He replied with the wry sense of humour I so admired in him, "Well, I realised one day that I was just kidding myself when I noticed that all my suicide plans were scuppered by thoughts like, 'Oh no, I can't possibly do it on Tuesday, my mum will find me,' and, 'It's my niece's birthday on Saturday, so not then – next week perhaps.' Then I realised that it was all in my mind and that there was no way I was going to kill myself. If you wanted to kill yourself, you'd just do it. No excuses."

This was a huge relief to hear and it also caused a small shift in me in that helped me to emerge slightly from my fog. I still lived with the relentless repetition of the PTSD symptoms – panicking at the sight or sound of an ambulance, having to check the children were breathing through the night, suddenly seeing Romy's dead body in front of me at random moments – but I started to respect the process my mind was going through.

I also began to search for something else to focus on. Reading, watching TV or anything requiring active engagement was impossible for me. I kept worrying that TV programmes would show the death of a baby or young child and I wouldn't be able to cope. My mind couldn't retain information very well so reading was a repetitive process. Social situations became minefields and I didn't know how people were expecting me to act so I simply avoided them. Overall, most things seemed so pointless to me, and other people's small talk and chat could quickly become incendiary. An innocent joke about feeling like death because her baby had kept her up all night made me want to punch another local mother. Hearing repeated good-natured complaints from parents about how long the summer holidays were was hard too. It was almost funny how often I began to hear total strangers quip things like, "Well, never mind if they're arguing, at least they're all still breathing!" Actually no, all my children weren't still breathing, and I was still having trouble not blaming myself for that one.

And so I returned to what had held me so many times before: Spiritualism and healing. Every Saturday evening I frequented my local Spiritualist church. I didn't have to tell anybody about Romy; in fact, I would arrive just before the service began to avoid interacting with anyone. I would sit at the back, join in with the uplifting songs to raise the energy vibration and week after week I received messages from mediums giving me snippets of information about my life, my loved ones in Spirit and, often, Romy. During these visits I heard details of how Romy passed, various family members she was with in the spirit world (my grandparents, my father-in-law, Darius's Aunt Jeannette). I was even told that one day I would be standing on a platform and helping others as I was being helped.

There were signs from Romy in those early days too. It has always been our habit to keep our babies with us as much as possible. Even at night we would alternate wearing them in a sling or carrier or wrap them up snugly next to us on the sofa as we watched TV. Each evening I would feed Romy and then pass her to Darius to hold while I went to prepare our dinner. She would sleep happily with us for the rest of the evening. As we prepared to go to bed I would go upstairs to check on the children and Darius would switch off the lights and carry Romy upstairs to join us. It became a little ritual that he would place her in our bed and come into the bathroom just as I was coming out to get into bed beside her.

For the first three nights after she died, I saw her, as clear as day, in our bed as I came out of the bathroom. The first time it was a shock and I thought that my mind was playing tricks on me. It was also dreadfully upsetting as the whole situation hit me afresh and I collapsed in tears, inconsolable at having to go to bed without my baby. On the second night I began to question my sanity but on the third, the image was even clearer and remained for longer than it had on the other two nights. To begin with, it had been a "blink and you'll miss it" image. I just thought I had caught sight of her out of the corner of my eye, I did a double take and she had gone. On the second night I thought I had a clearer view, but the third night was unmistakeable: her little head was there right next to my pillow as it had always been. I'm not sure whether this was what is sometimes referred to as an "imprint"; when the energy or emotion of a situation is so strong that it replays even after its protagonists are no longer on the earth plane. Whatever it was, I wasn't ready for it at all and tearfully asked Spirit to make it stop on the third night. As always, they listened, because I never saw Romy in our bed again.

When Darius and I arrived at the Harry Edwards Healing Sanctuary just ten days after Romy left us we were expecting simply to experience some kind of brief respite from the devastation of our grief. Such had been my distress when I called to book our appointments that they had assigned us two healers each and an extended session of one hour as opposed to thirty minutes. I collapsed on to the couch, desperate to escape the misery that was dragging me down and keen to let the healers do their work. I wasn't disappointed. Almost immediately I drifted off as I felt the warmth from their hands soothing my exhausted mind and aching limbs. I closed my eyes and allowed my mind to drift and became immediately aware of stone steps in front of me. I had seen these before, many years ago when I had got into the habit of listening to guided meditations as I went to sleep. One of the meditations had encouraged you to visualise steps going down into a garden as a technique of easing you into the exercise and each time I descended them I found myself in a small cottage garden that appeared to belong to my grandmother Sylvia. Each night I would meet her there and watch as she pottered among the blooms just as I remembered her doing when I was a child. She loved her garden and was forever taking me on tours of it, teaching me the names of all the plants and flowers she loved so much. As I descended the steps in my healing session the familiarity of this garden came as a surprise but I wasn't in the least bit surprised when out of the overflowing garden emerged my grandmother. I felt a rush of emotion as I saw her and she enveloped me in a warm hug.

As I stepped back from her embrace I saw my grandfather, Stuart, the man I had seen in my first ever spiritual visitation at the age of fourteen, and he was carrying Romy. I felt tears running down my cheeks but I didn't dare open my eyes in case the image disappeared. It might seem as if this was some kind of additional torture but the feelings I felt were pure love and relief. I was so happy to see my precious baby in the arms of my own loved ones and felt reassured that she was being taken care of. The scene remained for a few moments and I watched as my grandfather carried Romy into the beautiful garden where my grandmother greeted them among the flowers. I didn't want to come back.

Of course, the session came to an end and I rushed to meet Darius and tell him about my experience. It was a hot summer's day and we took our lunch and went to sit down on the lawns outside the healing rooms. A small waterfall was playing over some rocks and we simply lay down, held hands and felt the earth beneath our bodies and the sun above them. It was a beautiful moment of repose and one during which I feel that I began tentatively to rediscover my somewhat lost connection with Spirit. It was while we were lying on the ground that I told Darius that I thought there was another baby to come. This place felt like a portal to another world. It reignited my passion for the art of healing and gave me a direction. I still visit the sanctuary as often as I can and even wrote part of this book there. It has a unique and powerful energy.

Prompt: In a "dark night of the soul", how do you cope? Do you seek healing, and if so, in what form is that meaningful to you? Playing music? Gardening? Writing? Spending time with animals? Are your coping methods helpful for your soul's expansion, or do they cause it to shrink (e.g. getting drunk, ranting negatively about the situation, feeling sorry for yourself)?

Chapter 10

A Funny Thing Happened On the Way to the Morgue...

Laughter can shake you from the delirium of grief.
– **Lidia Yuknavitch**

Greek theatre teaches us that comedy and tragedy are inextricably linked. The emblem of the Greek masks reminds us that in the midst of our laughter may suddenly arrive a calamitous situation; and likewise while we grieve there may occur moments of pure comedy. Within a Greek drama there arrives a moment known as *peripeteia* which refers to the point at which the tragedy can't get any more tightly wound and something – sometimes a comic moment – occurs to loosen that knot and unwind everything. Tension is lifted and the characters in the drama are afforded a new understanding of the circumstances. If we think about this, what we are looking at is a moment of profound healing but our culture today does not feel comfortable acknowledging this. It's difficult enough for us to discuss death or the dying at all let alone laugh at, or about it. We probably have the Victorians to blame for this. Instigators of the "Keep Calm and Carry On" ethos, they shrouded anything they deemed unpalatable in mystery and drapes. They were masters of the art of pretence to such an extent that they took photographs of their deceased, propped up eerily next to living relatives in a creepy charade that attempted the illusion that they were still physically present. Surprisingly, the afterlife and spirit communication held intense fascination for the Victorians but this too was kept securely under wraps. The Greeks, on the other hand, approached the whole business of death and dying with earthiness. To them, death was simply a part of life and took its place alongside humour.

I began training as a healer during my first pregnancy and during bus journeys across London to visit various of my pregnant reflexology clients I would study and read books for my course. One of these books was *The NHS Healer* by Angie Buxton-King. Ironically I remember telling my mother that of all the things I could have chosen to read while pregnant, this would not have been something I would consciously have picked had I known the subject matter beforehand.

Angie writes about her son, Sam, who was diagnosed with leukaemia. Throughout Sam's many hospital stays and treatments, Angie was of course by his side. After a time she began to realise that the hand holding and head stroking that she was instinctively doing as a loving mother could perhaps be channelled even more proactively and she began to explore working with energy as a healer. She went on to give healing to many of Sam's friends on the children's cancer wards, to remarkable effect. Sam passed away but Angie's positivity allowed her to accept that the healing she had given to her son had immensely improved his quality of life and even extended it beyond the initial prognosis of his disease. She also had many grateful parents of other young patients at Great Ormond Street Hospital reinforce her belief that healing had a place in cancer wards; providing warmth, positivity, love and relief for those who struggle with its demands. As much as we have to thank modern medicine for – its ability to heal the ravages of disease and to give many thankful individuals more time with their families – there comes a point at which we may have to accept that an individual's path is to return home to Spirit rather than to remain here with us. If, like me, you believe that they chose this path in this lifetime to access learning then we can argue that nothing other than divine intervention of some sort can change this outcome. We grieve because we want their presence to continue alongside ours. We do not want to feel the gaping absence of those we love. But if it is their destiny, and even their choice, to return home to Spirit then we must respect this path. Being able to offer love and healing to those who struggle with the physical and emotional difficulties of disease without being attached to the outcome is a powerful gesture indeed, and teaches us much about love, understanding and deep spirituality. Something that has helped me enormously since having to accept the absence of my daughter's physical presence are the repeated suggestions that her non-physical presence is still very much alive. I feel it, I have seen it and I feel reassured and guided by it.

Angie's book made a huge impact on me and I devoured it within days, little knowing that a decade later I would come to know her personally. Angie's remarkable tribute to her son was to forge ahead with an initiative to train as many healers as possible to work within NHS hospitals and this movement is growing steadily. The Sam Buxton Sunflower Healing Trust part-funds many such positions within the UK's National Health Service and brings relief, peace and joy to many. So why does this heart-rending story find itself here in a chapter on humour in grief? Because many years later, after I too had experienced the loss of my child I had the good fortune to correspond with and then to learn from Angie and I found her to be a woman full of positivity and humour. From the first email response I received from her to the time I spent studying on her course I found her engaging personality and warmth to be immensely uplifting. It gave me hope that I could look forward to a future where I might be able to laugh, crack jokes and share my strength with others. Angie showed me that a bereaved mother does not need to be full of anger and self-recrimination or appear to be permanently downcast. Her zest for life and commitment to providing healing for as many cancer patients as possible, served with a healthy dose of sharp wit, made me realise that the best way we can honour our children is by living our lives as the best version of ourselves. Rather than living out the rest of our days as a shadow of our former self we can emerge as an enhanced, illuminated version of the person that our deceased loved ones knew here on earth.

During one session on Angie's course we discussed the importance of humour when working as a healer in palliative and end of life care. As Angie says, just because a person is dying, it doesn't mean you have to tiptoe around them or treat them like a saint. Sometimes, all they want is a good laugh. The same is true of the bereaved, and of those who sit at the bedside of a terminally ill loved one. There were some inescapably funny moments during our short time with Romy at the Paediatric Intensive Care Unit at King's, even in the hours directly following her death. It feels uncomfortable to relay this truth, but we laughed in that room, even though our child had just died. There was also a hilarious occurrence at the hospital mortuary two days later and we could feel laughter bubbling up at the funeral director's too. Laughter is a powerful emotional release. When we seek to connect to Spirit, laughter is also instrumental in raising the vibration to sufficiently high levels for them to communicate with us. We should not be afraid of laughter if it comes during a passing or afterwards. It is healing, and it allows us to feel close to our loved one who has passed, as well as to our fellow mourners. However difficult our internal struggle may be when we are grieving – and this is intensely personal from one person to the next – the shared joy of laughter cannot fail to connect us. I imagine that when my time comes and I pass to the spirit world I would be delighted if I could look down on my family and see and hear them laughing together, sharing stories and remembering me with love.

For me, during those two days of unbearable intensity and sadness, humour, when it came, provided a welcome relief from the constant adrenaline spikes and anxiety so heightened that I felt constantly nauseous. In the small room in which we sat with Romy as she took her last breaths there was laughter. Of course, there was also howling, wailing and sobbing but I can recall some moments of real beauty as we sat with Romy and listened as Kat, the wonderful nurse assigned to us, explained the order of things and what would happen to our precious daughter now that she was no longer physically with us. Kat brought us some scissors to take a lock of Romy's hair and we laughed as I insisted that I would be the one doing the cutting as I didn't trust Darius not to give our daughter a terrible haircut.

Days after we returned home we began planning Romy's remembrance ceremony, which included finding a final resting place for her. We had all our parents staying with us at the time and after a couple of trips to various woodland burial grounds we found a place that felt perfect and told everyone that we would like to take them up there one evening. It was important to us that the children and our parents had a chance to see the place we had chosen for Romy. As we prepared to get in the car Kasper asked where we were going. I said, "Well, we're going to see the place that Romy's body will be in when we have the special ceremony to remember her next week." Obviously in a state of some confusion over what had been explained to him concerning where we go after death Kasper ran back towards the house where his grandparents were exiting and called out excitedly, "Hurry up! We're all going to Heaven!"

We were committed to avoiding all conventional funeral traditions. It was important to us to remember our daughter with positivity, and also to create for her a remembrance service that would show our surviving children that death was nothing to be afraid of; that it was simply an onward journey. We wanted it to reflect our own particular spirituality and for it to be an appropriate place for our children to be with us. We knew that a traditional black hearse was out of the question but what alternative was there? One evening I sat and did some research on "alternative funeral vehicles" and the results threw up some very interesting finds, including articulated lorries, rickshaws and converted ice cream trucks. As I looked, I heard a voice say, "camper van," and I knew I'd struck gold. Kasper was at that time obsessed with vehicles and camper vans were one of his favourites. I looked at a website with some for hire and saw that the back shelf would provide an ideal place for Romy's woven willow casket while the rest of us could sit together. It was cheerful and colourful in an entirely respectful way and I loved the idea. Just at that moment Darius's sister Nuria happened to call and during the conversation expressed her very kind wish to contribute to Romy's ceremony. Without realising what I had just been doing, Darius spontaneously told her that we were having trouble deciding on an appropriate vehicle to carry her to the ceremony and that we had turned down the funeral director's offer of a hearse, meaning that we would need to source an alternative. Nuria was delighted to be able to help but her first question sent me into fits of laughter as she enquired as sensitively as she could but with obvious alarm, "It's not going to be an ice cream van, is it?"

In the end, we chose a burgundy-coloured classic camper van that the children loved and in which we all went camping on the night after the ceremony. More hilarity ensued during this, possibly the most bizarre family break I have ever taken in my life. As darkness set in, my paranoia about the children's safety had reached fever pitch and I persuaded Darius to block the entrance to the van by moving our tent in front of one of the doors, thereby foiling any attempts by predators to snatch our sleeping children. We are not experienced campers and as we scrambled about in the darkness cursing and tripping over tent pegs we slowly glanced up to see the rest of the campsite watching with amused interest from around their respective campfires. Of course, they were all kitted out with head torches and were far more adept than us at moving around in the pitch darkness. We began joking to each other in whispers that it was amateur night in our corner of the site and before we knew it we were laughing hysterically at our efforts.

After we had calmed down and sat under the stars I did have a moment when I asked myself whether we were out of our minds, taking our children camping when we had just buried our daughter, but I felt a sense of calm wash over me as I recalled watching our older children scampering about the campsite earlier in the evening, making friends and being excited about sleeping in the van. We had done the right thing for our family. We could be sitting at home crying, our children could feel bewildered and afraid but instead we were outside in the fresh air, surrounded by nature, creating a positive family experience; a contrast from the sadness that had engulfed our house just days before.

The seminal comic moment that remains with me involves our visit to the hospital mortuary. After an unspeakably awful weekend at home it struck me as both morbid and bizarre that on the Monday I felt practically ebullient at the thought of travelling back up to London to visit Romy. I was appalled at myself as I realised that I was excited about going to visit the body of my daughter, but I missed her so terribly that even the thought of being able to hold her, kiss her and change her into her own clothes was one that I found cheering. I had it in my mind that I wanted to give Romy a last bath, change her out of the borrowed hospital Babygro (her clothes had had to be cut off by the paramedics at home) and into her own clothes, brush her hair and perform the last duties of care that I could as her mother.

The walk from the hospital reception area to the mortuary was excessively long and seemed to traverse a never-ending trail of corridors. At some point during it we found ourselves walking behind a prison guard handcuffed to a prisoner. What they were doing heading for the morgue we had no idea but as Darius muttered, "You couldn't make this up!" we struggled to contain our sniggers. We were met at the doors to the mortuary and shown inside to where Romy lay in a Moses basket, balanced on top of one of those wooden stands that usually accompany them. From the first hours after she was born Romy slept in our bed, on top of one of us on the sofa or in a sling so it was alien to see her lying in any kind of cot or basket. It was overwhelmingly terrible to see our child like that and we both collapsed, sobbing, into the chairs next to the basket. We were left alone for a few moments, during which time Darius tried to move closer to Romy to talk to her by leaning on the side of the basket frame. "For God's sake don't lean on that, you'll have the whole thing over!" I hissed at him. Darius can be clumsy at the best of times and the mental image of him collapsing on top of the whole structure and us then having to explain ourselves to someone suddenly struck us both as hilarious.

We were desperately trying to collect ourselves when the mortuary assistant assigned to us walked in to introduce herself. I try not to have any preconceived ideas about anyone in any situation but I have to confess that this lady challenged my ability to see past the outer layers. She was of a reasonably large build, dressed in black jeans and a black T-shirt, with barely contained wild curly hair and tattoos over every available surface of visible skin. To top it all, she had multiple piercings in her ears and nose. I have to say that she had an incredibly kind face and manner and was clearly adept at her job of putting her clients at ease and gently talking them through the gruelling business of caring for one's deceased loved one. As she spoke to introduce herself, however, something terrible happened.

"Hello," she announced gravely, "I'm Jeannette."

Time froze. We didn't dare look at each other. Already exhausted from my attempts to stifle my giggles I couldn't cope with the prospect of having to do it all over again, this time with the subject of our mirth standing right in front of us, sitting in front of our daughter's body. My hysterics were caused by the fact that I just couldn't shake the thought that, of all the people to share a name with our dear recently departed Aunt Jeannette (and Jeannette is not a common name), this lady couldn't have looked more different. The Aunt Jeannette we all knew and loved was glamorous, always impeccably turned out, didn't care for tattoos or piercings and would never have been seen in such casual attire, dead or otherwise. The words, "My God! I would never have thought you'd choose to come back like *this*!" popped into my head and it was all I could do not to blurt them out. What was worse was that I absolutely knew that Darius was having exactly the same thought. It was just too much. I have no idea how we got through those long minutes without embarrassing ourselves but can only hope that the strange choking noises we emitted as we clutched at each other must have been assumed to be the ravings of two grief-stricken parents.

As it turned out, my plans to change Romy's clothes and bathe her did not come to fruition. Once my attack of the giggles had subsided the enormity of what I intended to do dawned on me and I just couldn't do it. Even now, admitting that fact fills me with shame. I so desperately wanted to perform this last service for my daughter in a way that continues a ritual known to our ancestors for generations but when it came to it – and I know this sounds ridiculous – I was terrified that I might break her in some way. Jeannette the mortuary assistant embodied all that was loving and proactive about her namesake as she carefully washed and dressed our daughter for us because, in the depths of my grief, I could not.

If you yourself have a loved one or loved ones in Spirit you will know that grief is a grim rollercoaster that throws you around with relentless speed. You are either the person pretending that everything is okay while silently screaming inside, or you are consumed with your own imploding anger at everyone and everything because the force that took your loved one away is so unfair. In grief, life is unfair, nothing has meaning and everybody else's pathetic existences are meaningless; their perceived problems, nothing.

As we navigate these waters it is vital to recognise the role of humour. Our culture takes a sharp intake of breath at the thought of laughing in the face of death, or even afterwards at a funeral or wake, but in some communities this is entirely acceptable. The Irish come to mind as they take great pride in burying their dead with deep respect and faith before heading to the nearest drinking establishment for a knees-up, a laugh and a joke while remembering their dearly departed with humour and love. To me, this attitude is healthy and necessary. I'm not suggesting that anyone needs to imbibe alcohol at a funeral; rather that the collective gathering to enjoy food, company and merriment is a healthy expression of our grief. It is possible to relax and act exactly as our loved one might wish us to do with them if they were here. It is we who impose the rules of mourning; who decide that any expression of mirth is disrespectful.

I read a eulogy at Romy's ceremony. It was very important to me that our surviving children saw me stand up in front of our loved ones with my head held high, speaking clearly about the blessing of Romy. I did not want them to see me slumped in a chair crying inconsolably – they had seen enough of that at home. At this very public expression of our gratitude, love and grief I wanted them to see strength. During the eulogy I thanked Darius for his grace, strength and love but in the interests of complete honesty I also confided in the congregation that he was the most intensely annoying person I have ever known. I am sure that the resounding laughter with which that comment was met was tinged with relief. People were so grateful to have the opportunity to release some emotion through laughter rather than tears.

I was genuinely happy to witness several other small moments of comic relief during the ceremony. Our dear friend David, a former professional opera singer who had flown home from a big family celebration in Italy especially to perform a particular song for Romy, inadvertently supplied one of them. As a hush befell the small service hall in preparation for his highly emotional unaccompanied solo he suddenly whipped out his mobile phone and started fiddling about with the screen. There was some shifting in seats and a sense of puzzled expectation. Realising that all eyes were on him, he announced in his fantastically resonant stage voice, "Sorry, I'm not doing my email, I need to find the right note to tune up my voice and I have an App to do that with." Right at the end of the ceremony we had asked our friend Chris to press "play" on the CD player at the front, which was loaded with an album by Seal. Being a CD, alas it wasn't possible to tee up the correct track (we had chosen *Kiss from a Rose*), and in his haste to get the song started at the right moment Chris simply hit "play" without thinking to check which track was showing on the digital display. Unfortunately, the song at the beginning of the album began with a voice screaming the words, "Bring it on!" with great gusto; and this just as we were preparing to file out to the graveside for the burial. Poor Chris was mortified but we were so grateful for this moment of release. It felt so good to see that we had created an environment in which we could honour our daughter and in which our friends and loved ones could feel relaxed enough to laugh in our presence. Hearing that laughter was a healing balm to us and so much more uplifting a sound than that of tears.

It cannot be denied that death and dying produce moments of utter hilarity; total howlers that serve to help us to release pent-up emotion and nervous energy and to bond with our family, friends and loved ones. Sometimes it is just a relief to do something other than cry. Mere days after Romy left us, I called my friend Natasha and asked if I could see her. She and I had known each other through our children for a couple of years and got on well, but it was during my pregnancy with Romy and after her passing that we became close friends. It was Natasha who helped me to make a belly cast just a few weeks before Romy was born. The whole process was hilariously funny, as Natasha tiptoed around in her underwear to avoid getting plaster of Paris on her jeans, wrapping me in clingfilm and wet strips of plaster-covered bandage. All the while we were both eating chocolate biscuits and navigating an awkward exchange with our postman who rang the doorbell trying to deliver a parcel just at a crucial moment.

After days of uncontrollable sobbing and utter desperation it was Natasha I wanted to speak to. I called her and asked her to come round so we could go for a walk together. "I just need to get out of this house and to be honest I need a bloody good laugh," I told her. She herself is no stranger to unexpected loss and I knew that she would understand exactly what I meant.

We found ourselves in a field somewhere at the back of my house, struggling through the long grass and laughing until our sides ached as I regaled her with the mortuary assistant story. I had brought along with me one cigarette and a foldover pack of matches, in which two or three were left. I had smoked many years ago and given up long before we had children. I had also given up alcohol and become a vegetarian at around the same time. In the days that followed Romy's death I momentarily returned to all these former habits; largely because I just didn't know what to do with myself and smoking, drinking and breaking as many rules as I could without endangering myself or others seemed to provide some kind of outlet, although the effects were brief. I am not proud to admit that I received no less than three speeding tickets in two weeks, which resulted in my attendance at a speed awareness course. I had driven too fast on three visits up to the burial ground, blinded by tears, alone in the car and battling with dark thoughts. As I sank to the ground and attempted to light my one cigarette I blew through all three matches. For a moment I stared at Natasha in blind incomprehension. How could life be so cruel? I had just lost my child, I was trying my best to do something reckless in protest and The Universe had seen fit to blow out not one, but three matches? We both burst out laughing at the ridiculousness of the situation, and again, the release felt good.

To the Spirit world, laughter is sacred. When we laugh, we lift our energy and that of those around us. Laughter also raises the energetic vibration enough for those in Spirit to draw close to us. Recent years have seen the rise in popularity of "laughter yoga", during which participants sit in the same room as someone who begins to laugh spontaneously and consistently. As we all know, when someone close by is genuinely laughing and especially if they are unable to control themselves, it is impossible not to join in with at least a smile. Eventually, the whole room is laughing and it creates a unique bond between all those present. Laughter is contagious because its energy is pure and positive.

I am reminded of a time when I was giving a reflexology treatment to my mother. She's not a huge fan of massage but she was happy to receive reflexology from me and had drifted off into a light sleep. Before we began the treatment we had been laughing and joking together about something or other and midway through the session, after she had closed her eyes to relax, I heard, clear as a bell, her father's – my grandfather's – voice. It was so clear it was as if someone had switched on a radio. I heard a few swallowed words, as if he were telling the punchline to a joke, followed by a burst of his instantly recognisable laughter. My grandfather was known for his upbeat nature and easy humour so the fact that I had heard him joking and laughing felt entirely natural and believable to me. What's more, when my mother woke after the session and I told her what I had heard, she replied that she had had a sense of her father standing next to her as she lay on the bed.

Laughter is a form of release and there is no need to suppress it before, during or after a death just because our social conditioning tells us that it's somehow inappropriate or disrespectful. Personally, I'd be delighted if attendees at my funeral were in gales of laughter. Seeing the humour in any situation, particularly challenging ones, can give us clearer perspective and remind us that maybe it's not as bad as we're telling ourselves it is. And when we allow laughter to creep in to our grief we can feel closer to our loved ones, both living and passed.

Prompt: In a challenging situation, can you connect with humour? Does your focus go to anxiety and panic, or are you able to step aside and look for the funny side? This can work even in extreme situations (note: it happened to me in a morgue).

Chapter 11

Messages From Romy

What we have once enjoyed, we can never lose. All that we love deeply becomes a part of us.
– Helen Keller

With all that I have experienced from the world of Spirit and all that I believe, if you think I accepted the incidents I'm about to describe to you without question then you'd be wrong. I found it very difficult to connect with any of my Spiritual beliefs immediately following Romy's passing, to the extent that when I look back on these accounts now it amuses me to think that Spirit – and Romy – were practically banging me over the head trying to get my attention. Eventually I sought out mediums in an attempt to try and make some kind of contact and many of those encounters corroborated the things I am about to tell you.

I respect anyone's ideas or belief system when it comes to life after death and the spirit world; however, to me, these events happened and they are real. I am not seeking to convert anyone to my way of thinking when I tell them; I do so because they are uplifting and inspirational to me and have given me an enormous amount of hope. To me, the experiences I'm going to describe are absolutely true, and they began within weeks of Romy's passing.

Sometime in mid-August 2014, things were really bad. As anyone who grieves or has grieved will tell you, there is an in-between space after loss. When a loved one passes, those around us gather close. We experienced overwhelming kindness from family, friends and those in our small village community, who rallied to provide as much support and help as they could muster. This touched us greatly and Darius and I will never forget the beauty of sitting together every evening to talk, cry and laugh over a lovingly prepared meal delivered to our door by friends, neighbours and, in some cases, total strangers. I didn't cook for a month and it gave the two of us time and space to be close to each other, to share our feelings, to be with our children and talk about Romy. However, after a time people started to drift away, to merge back in to their own lives and this is absolutely natural. It wouldn't be right to expect anyone to constantly sit and hold our hand through our grief as some of it is deeply personal and may only be able to be expressed when we are alone. For this reason, we sometimes fear being alone as the intensity of that grief, when it comes, can feel overwhelming. For me, the shock of the experience reverberated for many months to come (my mother says that I wasn't anything like myself for at least eighteen months) and around a month after Romy passed, I fell into a very dark place.

In those days I spent a lot of time sitting by Romy's resting place. I felt so lost and confused; in my turmoil I held the belief that she wasn't there in that spot but at times my grief-addled brain imagined all sorts of awful images when I looked at the tiny little mound of earth. And yet, it was the place I felt closest to her. By making time to go and sit there I also felt that I was making time for her in my life, just as I would if she were physically present. Once Macsen arrived it became very difficult to visit each week and it took me a long time to reconcile myself to this fact.

One morning that August I was having a particularly bad day. With weary resignation I recognised on waking that that day was going to be a tough one, and rather than fight it, I gave in. I decided to go and sit with Romy and cry for a while. I arrived at the woodland burial ground and began the walk through the trees towards Romy's spot. We had deliberately avoided placing her in the so-called "baby glade" as oddly, to us, she didn't seem like a baby. I have often thought that this shows that I somehow knew from the outset that Romy was an older, more experienced soul. She never seemed "new". I arrived at her grave and collapsed on to the grass in the warm sunshine. I cast a quick glance about me to check for other mourners as in typically British fashion I didn't want to risk alarming anyone else with my display of grief. The place was empty, which is what I would have expected at 10am on a weekday morning in high summer.

It felt strange to be feeling so unutterably desperate and low in such a beautiful environment. The sun was warm on my face, birds were singing in the trees and the grass was brilliant green. This only made me feel worse and I gave in to my grief and started to howl. I felt so awful I couldn't even try to control myself as I usually did; I just lay on the grass and screamed and cried. I have no idea how long I carried on like this but I do know that at some point I yelled something like, "For God's sake, somebody help me! I can't go on. Please, help me!"

At that moment, something shifted. When I say that I was lying on the floor screaming and howling I am not exaggerating but at that moment I stopped dead in my tracks because I felt what I can only describe as a presence. The energy had changed, not imperceptibly but dramatically. It was now impossible to scream or cry because something was in front of me commanding my attention and when I raised my head to look I couldn't believe my eyes.

In front of me, to the far left corner of Romy's grave was a column of electric blue light. It was cylindrical in shape, around six or seven feet tall and wide enough to fit an adult inside. No pantone sheet in the world could accurately describe the exact nature of the blue colour. It was electric blue, cobalt blue, cornflower blue but it wasn't a static mass; it shimmered and shifted with silver light and looked alive and incandescent. It was not of this world. As I stared in silent disbelief, I began to make out that this wasn't a singular presence, but a multitude. It felt like a group of people with Romy somewhere among them. This collective energy felt so familiar, like walking into a room full of your closest family and friends; the people you love and cherish most in the world. I don't know how long I sat in front of that column of light. If I try to attribute a timescale to the experience I would say it was around five minutes or so but it literally felt as if time had stood still. I didn't say anything, I didn't hear anything but it was as if the column of light was able to communicate to me directly without the use of language or words; like a form of mental telepathy. I received an impression of the words, "All is well. We are with you." Then the column of blue light faded fairly rapidly and I sat very still for several moments trying to make sense of what I had just seen. I suddenly noticed that I had stopped crying and felt an overwhelming peacefulness and calm.

Can I find a logical explanation for this account? I can have a good try. I was tired, overwrought, probably so grief-stricken I was prone to hallucination. I've read books about spiritual happenings and simply imagined the whole episode. Perhaps my mind played a trick on me. Maybe, while at my lowest ebb emotionally, my brain conjured up some imagery to help me to release my grief. I am open to accepting all these as possibilities but my inner voice, my intuition, gives me a different explanation. At first I thought I had seen an angel, and for a while afterwards I would refer to the experience as The Blue Angel, but this never felt quite right due to the fact that I had so clearly felt the presence of many, rather than one. Also, the words impressed upon me were, "... We are with you." I instinctively felt that I had somehow met my soul group.

My understanding is that we are all part of one consciousness in Spirit but that within that whole there exist many soul groups. These are comprised of a number of souls who wish to incarnate and learn together on earth. Have you ever met someone and felt certain that you've known them before? Some believe that you have indeed done so, perhaps in many previous lifetimes in different relationships. So for example, in one lifetime your brother with whom you fought over land ownership might turn up in this life as an overbearing boss. Gender can change, so your sister in this life might have been your father previously. This is a vast topic but for those who are interested there are many excellent books on the subject of reincarnation including fascinating case histories: Dr Brian Weiss' *Many Lives, Many Masters* and *Other Lives, Other Selves* by Roger Woolger to name but two. Shortly after I had this experience Darius and I met with Michelle's friend Jan, who corroborated my feelings during our sitting with her.

A few weeks after the encounter with the blue light I was at home alone during the day. After a brief period of time when I decided that I had to start looking for a new job, I realised that I was in no fit state to work. My assertion a few weeks before Romy passed that I would not be working with reflexology or birth any more had turned out to be correct. At that time I assumed it was because coming into contact with pregnancy or babies would be too painful. I also worried that if I were ever to work with a couple who experienced miscarriage or stillbirth it would only bring up all my own issues and I wouldn't be able to cope, or to help them. I realise now that I knew before Romy died that my time doing that work was finished; I had, after all, made a promise to Spirit. On a deep level, I was recognising and being true to my blueprint, my plan.

At home one day browsing the Internet I came across the page of Carly Marie Dudley, an artist in Australia who produces beautiful beach artwork created in the sand in memory of babies and children who have passed. Each year she holds a beach remembrance ceremony, films it and posts it to her Facebook page and it's a very moving spectacle. I selected her video, started to play it and was pleased to find that the accompanying music was an instrumental piece from the film *Gladiator*. I was so moved to hear this evocative music that I wandered into our conservatory so I could look out at the part of our garden that contained Romy's memorial trees and rose bushes. I wanted to think of her as I listened. So hauntingly beautiful was the music that I was suddenly overcome with sadness. I was standing near a spot in the conservatory where we used to put Romy's baby chair; right next to the place where Darius would work when at home. She would sit bouncing alongside him happily, smiling and cooing at him. I have a treasured photograph of Darius holding Romy, a few hours old, in that very place with Kasper and Layla standing proudly alongside. I couldn't stop the tears from coming and as I rested my head against the windowpane I felt a presence in the room. I kept my eyes closed for a moment while I tried to place the feeling, asking myself whether the emotion of the music could be conjuring up an atmosphere and whether or not I was imagining it. Despite asking myself these questions I was certain that I was feeling Romy's presence, and it was filling up the room. It was like turning up a dial on the radio from soft to full volume: what began as a hint of a feeling very quickly became overwhelmingly "loud". I couldn't ignore it – my daughter was right there with me. I was still standing facing away from the room with my eyes closed but something told me to turn around and look, and when I did, there she was. I saw her, in her chair, on that spot, as clearly as I could see the furniture in the room, just for a few seconds, and then, as the song finished playing, she was gone.

To those of you who may be asking yourselves how a small baby could have the wherewithal to appear to me, or to fill a room with her presence, I ask you to remember that Romy's soul, or spirit, is distinct from her earthly body. Wherever she is now, in the spirit world, she no longer exists as Romy Norell but as a soul who forms part of a collective consciousness, as we all do once we return home to Spirit. However, our souls recognise that she is known to me as Romy, my child in this lifetime, so she may choose to appear to me in that form to give me comfort in that familiarity and to show me that she continues to exist.

By January 2015, we had our house on the market and the big change in our lives was in full swing. We had spent the previous months agonising over whether or not we should consider having another child. I was torn on the subject and could see us in either situation; Darius was unsure as to whether he could go through the worry of a pregnancy and having a tiny baby to look after again. We were both terrified at putting ourselves in a vulnerable position where, God forbid, we could experience further loss. One morning, I awoke with a clear sense of direction. I immediately turned to Darius and said, "I know you're not sure about another baby and I promise you that if you don't want to go ahead then I'm with you. But I have to tell you that I had a dream last night and I've woken up feeling that there's another child for us. I think, if we ask this child to join us, they will." To my amazement, Darius replied telling me that he too had had a vivid dream and had woken up feeling the same. Within a week or two, I was pregnant with our son Macsen.

Dreams are an easy way for Spirit to communicate with us as we experience them when our brain is in a supremely relaxed and receptive state. This state most often occurs just before we drop off to sleep and also just before our consciousness fully kicks in when we wake up. It is the same state we experience when we meditate, and in which we can receive communication from Spirit as the logical, neocortex part of the brain is not butting in with questions and interruptions. If impressions come to us in dreams, when we wake and start to process them it can become easy to dismiss our journeyings as "just a dream". But are they?

Somewhere around this time I had an extraordinary dream that has remained vivid in every detail since. In it, I was floating face down in water; not in an alarming way, but feeling a calm sense of just being held by the water. I had no sense of urgency, no inclination to move, I was just suspended there. I became aware of a voice talking to me. It sounded muffled, like being in the bath and submerging yourself in the water so that sounds and voices above the surface take on an otherworldly quality. I tried to make out some words but was immediately struck by the familiarity of the voice – it was mine! This was confusing. How could I be talking to myself while suspended in water? I listened closely and began to make out parts of speech. "Go to the light… they are all waiting for you… Mummy and Daddy love you very much." I couldn't believe it; I was hearing the exact words I had uttered to Romy as she passed.

I had a momentary sense of trepidation that I liken to the feeling I once experienced as a child on a high diving board. Aged nine or ten I had told my father I wanted to jump off the high board at our local swimming pool during our weekend visit there, and as he watched me, I climbed the steps up. Once I got to the top and there was a queue of people forming behind me I realised that I had to jump. I really, really wanted to jump: in fact, I had spent many weeks enviously watching other children leaping off the top board, but when it came to that moment I was petrified. I knew that, for me, backing out wasn't an option so for just a few seconds I was frozen there until, eventually, I screwed up my courage and jumped. In my dream, I experienced that same feeling for a fleeting moment before I let go.

In this "dream" I was, in fact, Romy. The feeling of being suspended in water was a representation of being in a comatose state. I was detached from my physical body but conscious on a deep level. As Romy, I could hear my own voice, telling me that everything was okay, that I could go towards the light. At that moment, I experienced a feeling of letting go amidst an exhilarating surge of energy. I registered the thought, "This is it! I know everything! It's all so simple!" and felt the energy pull strongly upwards. At that moment, back in our house, Layla woke suddenly and called out for me. I leapt out of bed to go to her and when I returned to our bed I was still completely awestruck by what I had just experienced. I woke Darius and told him, "I've just dreamed about Romy. She showed me what it was like to die."

And that is exactly what I believe that incident was. I believe that I was shown just enough to convince me of the validity of my experience but that the scene was cut short deliberately (by Layla waking suddenly) as it was not deemed necessary or appropriate for me to be given any further knowledge. Why was I shown it? I'm not sure, but around that time I had been consumed with irrational worries about whether or not Romy had been in any pain and I feel that this was a reassurance by her that she was not. I also believe that I was given a privileged insight into the process of death as experienced by my daughter, to help me in my path.

In the months after Romy passed and the children returned to school, I struggled. Socialising with anyone bar those who knew me very well was completely exhausting, and with no work to focus my overactive mind on, I was constantly falling prey to bouts of depression. Darius suggested that I go into town and have a relaxing treatment at a local beauty salon. I opted for a facial. I had spent so many hours crying in the past weeks that the idea of my face receiving some positive, nurturing attention seemed wonderful. I had very quickly learned how to negotiate situations like this as a bereaved parent. Situations involving simple small talk, such as introducing yourself to a therapist and settling into a treatment, can become fraught with difficulty. I managed to tell the therapist about Romy within five minutes of my arrival, thus sidestepping any potentially upsetting questions about the number of children I had, whether I might be pregnant and if I'd had a nice summer. It also achieved the effect of rendering the poor woman pretty much speechless (another common reaction), which was fine by me as all I wanted to do was zone out.

Soft music was playing in the room and as I relaxed into

the massage couch I began to breathe deeply and drift off into sleep. As I did so, I became aware of images forming on my "cinema screen". I seemed to be in a field sitting on the brightest green, springy grass underneath the canopy of a huge tree with spreading branches bursting with flowers and leaves. In all my visions of the spirit world I have been astounded at how green the grass is. I've never seen anything like it, and it has persisted in all the various scenarios I have experienced. Dotted around in the grass were the most stunning flowers I have ever seen. The overall picture was a little confusing as the field felt very much like one you would find in England on a summer's day, and yet the flowers growing in it were not the delicate countryside type you might expect but tall, exotic blooms in a variety of kaleidoscopic colours. I felt very much as I had during my past life regression years before: I was observing the scene while still being very much present within it. I looked down and saw that I was wearing a flowing white garment of some kind. I felt relaxed, happy and at peace, which highlighted to me just how low I had been recently. My grief had temporarily been lifted from my shoulders and I felt free and full of joy. I turned to my right and noticed a small child just next to me. I knew immediately, and without a shadow of a doubt, that this was Romy. She was standing, albeit on wobbly legs, and just about starting to take steps. Romy would have been around ten months old at this point and I knew that she was appearing to me just as she would have been had she still been here on earth. Her hair had grown a little and she was also wearing white. Our eyes connected, she half stumbled enthusiastically towards me and fell into my lap. As I threw my arms around her and held her close, I knew that this was a real experience. Tears streamed down my face and I could physically feel her body melting into mine. It was such a powerful connection and I never wanted it to end. But of course, end it did.

Several months later, in March 2015 I returned for another

treatment. Romy's birthday was coming up (alongside my own) and I wanted to see whether the relaxed state I achieved in the treatment room might enable me to reconnect with her again. This time, it took me a while to get to that particular state as my mind was whirring, asking if I was crazy, wondering whether anything would happen and trying not to force the issue in any way. Eventually I took some deep breaths and a scene began to unfold. I saw myself at the base of a steep hill. At its summit was a large tree and standing next to the tree was a small child: Romy. I began to walk up the hill and as I did so I noticed another figure. To my surprise, I recognised her as a spirit guide I had seen on many occasions when working with my pregnant clients. I had come to think of her as a type of midwife, but I have never been able to fathom which culture or period of time she might be from. She's a fairly short, stout lady with dark skin and she wears a type of white sari-like garment that winds about her body and is tied somewhere around it or underneath. She has an unusual white headdress that stands up in a triangular shape with two pointed corners above the ears. I have seen her standing next to pregnant clients as I've given them reflexology, and sometimes at births I have attended as a doula. As my vision adjusted to look at her more closely I saw that she had in her arms a small baby, which I knew to be a boy. I was just a few weeks pregnant with Macsen at the time and I knew that this "spiritual midwife" was presenting him to me, alongside Romy. I took this as a message that Romy was sending him to me.

The last story I will share here is one that occurred late in 2015, just after Macsen had arrived with us. Sitting up late one night feeding him, I was enjoying the peace and quiet and taking the chance to read a book. I happened to be reading about spirit communication and had just reached a part explaining how Spirit can often create electrical disturbances as a way of getting our attention and letting us know they are around. Macsen finished feeding and dropped off to sleep. As he was still very little it was my habit to make a mental note of the time he started and finished feeds to get a better idea of his schedule so I turned to look at the bedside clock to check the time. We have one of those alarm clocks that has a bedside light capable of illuminating gradually to mimic the sun rising in the morning; the idea being that you wake up in alignment with your body's Circadian rhythms. Underneath the light function is a digital clock and the whole unit is plugged in and runs from the electrical outlet in the bedroom. It does not have any batteries. We had rearranged the bedroom furniture just before Macsen was born, knowing that I would need to be next to the light while breastfeeding. I had checked the bulb and plug at the time so as not to find myself caught out without a clock or a nightlight and they were both in perfect working order.

As I broke off reading to check the time, to my dismay the clock blinked and went blank before my eyes. I looked closer. No, definitely no clock. How was this possible? The clock ran off the same electricity supply as the attached light, which was blazing brightly. Just as I was contemplating jumping out of bed to start messing around with the plug, the clock blinked back on again. The time was 11:11pm and to me, this was no coincidence; in fact, it was a powerful message. In numerology, the number 1 is considered a "master numeral" of great power and consequently any repeating patterns of 1 are regarded as very auspicious spiritually. In fact, many people recognise 1, 11 and 111 as Angelic numbers, or energy gateways to Spirit communication. To me, this was a clear message from Spirit. What better way to illustrate a capability to create electrical disturbances than to do so when I was in the middle of reading about that very phenomenon? Just in case I was going to try and dismiss it, Spirit threw in a highly significant time – 11:11 – just to make sure that I was paying proper attention.

These are just a selection of the experiences I have had and to me they illustrate that Romy – or, more precisely, her soul – continue on in the spirit world and that it is possible to communicate with her.

Prompt: Have you ever found yourself randomly thinking about a loved one who has passed? Do these thoughts pop into your head as you are going about your usual business? Do unusual things happen on their birthday or anniversary or when you are feeling low and missing them? This does not have to take the form of a column of blue light, it can be something seemingly insignificant that means something to you and the person you love. Common symbols from Spirit include particular birds or animals appearing whenever you think of that person, a song that you associate with them coming on to the radio or smelling their perfume, aftershave or favourite food unexpectedly. Pay attention to these signs: the more you do, the more you become attuned to your loved ones in Spirit trying to reach out to you.

Chapter 12

A Touch of Spirit

Close both eyes to see with the other.
– Rumi

I will begin this chapter by being up front. This is not one of those books where I tell you that before the death of my daughter I was a hardened journalist/brilliant scientist/person who just didn't have any time for spiritual mumbo jumbo. The Spiritualist stuff has been in my life right from the outset. In many ways it was a part of my upbringing and I have had experiences with "The Other Side" from as early on as I can remember.

Aside from the experiences that came to me personally after Romy's death I also, over time, began to seek communication from Spirit by visiting my local Spiritualist church where mediums were giving platform demonstrations. I also had sittings with three different mediums in private, one of whom knew me personally. Not only did these visits give me additional messages and information from Romy and other loved ones in spirit, they also independently corroborated some of the things I had experienced in private. The amount of crossover is such that I really came to trust my theories about why Romy was here, what I am set to learn from the experience and how I must use it to help others in their understanding and spiritual growth. I hope that reading these accounts proves as fascinating and helpful to others as being on the receiving end of the information was to me.

I am not going to write about a mind-blowing experience with a medium that changed my life forever or cured my scepticism. As a medium myself, I have a variety of tests and questions that I pose in order to feel confident that what I am receiving is a message from a spirit communicator and not a figment of my imagination or memory fragment from a film I have seen or a book I have read. Contrary to what you might expect, I am a person of common sense and always seek a logical explanation for what I see, hear or sense. After over forty years of being on this earth and receiving communication from Spirit I am gradually learning to trust what they give me, however outlandish it may at first appear. I have learned that it is often the simplest images, symbols or pieces of information that mean the most. I have also learned that if the image I see or fragment of music I hear persists then I can take it as spirit communication. All mediums work differently but what years of practice teach us is to trust our own translation skills. Spirit works very hard to give us information that will make sense to earthly loved ones and it is our job simply to communicate that information in the best way that we can.

I have been on the receiving end of many readings, sittings and communications with a reasonably large array of mediums both professional and non-professional over the course of some twenty-five years. I have also given sittings to others as a medium. From either side I have observed how tempting it is to come to a sitting with high expectations. If we are missing a particular loved one then it can be disappointing not to hear from them. Sometimes, we receive a message or information from a random spirit communicator whom we feel we did not know well on earth or perhaps we even disliked them. As a medium, we so want to help our sitter to connect with their loved one and we can also experience a very human fear of "getting it wrong"; of not being believed or taken seriously.

The simple truth that I have come to know is that Spirit will almost always connect you with the individual(s) and the information that *you most need to hear at that time*. No medium has a hotline to the spirit world, and however much we may wish we could, we cannot conjure up particular communicators.

We can ask, but we may only receive what is intended for us or our sitter to hear. Once we receive, it falls to our powers of translation to communicate that information to our sitter in a way that is meaningful to them. As I visited Spiritualist churches and mediums in the months after Romy died I can honestly say that it was never my intention solely to connect with my daughter. In a way, I felt that I already did this in my own, personal ways: taking flowers to her resting place each week, talking to her photograph, making a dedicated space for her in our garden. I sought out these places and people because I wanted to make sense of my grief and to reconnect with the spirit world. I was searching for hope: that my life had not ceased to be and that I could find purpose in it once again. The messages and information I received from Romy and other loved ones were heart-warming and uplifting but they were not my motivation. I wanted to find out how I could continue to live my life and rediscover my purpose rather than sinking into the despair of a life devoid of hope.

There are plenty of books written by established mediums that explain very well how mediumship works, but from my own experience I can say that when we tune into Spirit, the communication we receive can take a variety of different forms. I predominantly "see" information, as I have described, on a sort of cinema screen on the back of my forehead, behind my eyes. Sometimes this takes the form of recognisable people, places or objects; sometimes it takes the form of a scene being played out like a film; sometimes it's accompanied by a fragment of sound. I occasionally get a particular physical feeling with the information but sometimes, for no apparent reason whatsoever, all I will see is a random object or symbol and it then falls to me to attempt to interpret what it is I am seeing and translate it into a piece of information that is irrefutably correct and meaningful to my sitter. I believe that this is where sitters may find cause to come away feeling confused or disappointed, or even convinced that psychics and mediums are all frauds. There is a particular art in translating the information you are given by Spirit, preferably with no input from your sitter, and this takes experience gained from practice and time.

I believe that we are all born with the ability to tune in to this extra sixth sense, but that the majority of people are discouraged from doing so early in their lives when they are told that they have an overactive imagination or are accused of telling fibs or being silly. We all come from the same place: a place where communication is founded on a kind of telepathy, a "knowing" that doesn't require verbal communication, so it stands to reason that we would all come into this life with our sixth sense fully working and intact. We have created a society that doesn't tolerate this to the point that those of us who have hung on to this sense, developed it and hope to use it to help others are described as having a "gift". It is a gift, but one that we are all blessed with. It's just a question of whether or not we choose to see it and welcome it into our lives.

A good medium should not need to ask questions; neither should they attempt to backtrack or offer excuses or explanations for a piece of information that may appear to be wrong. All too often I have given information that has not been understood by my sitter only to find that, several weeks later, it has suddenly slotted into place. If Spirit gives us information it is our duty to pass it on as clearly and accurately as we can for the highest good of the recipient and if it is not understood we need to trust that, in time, it will be. I believe that some mediums quickly become unstuck in their entirely well-meaning attempts to provide something meaningful for their sitter, who may be grieving or looking for answers. Standing your ground and refusing to change the information you have been given, all the while ensuring that your delivery is sensitive and discreet, is a tough line to walk, but this is the way it has to be done. My dear friend and mentor Gerrie March taught me this. A wonderful medium of many years' standing, Gerrie hails from the North of England and has a warm, humorous and no-nonsense approach that endeared her to me from the start of my training with her back in 2001. I sat in circle with Gerrie for several years, eventually taking part in one or two demonstrations of mediumship. I was at the point when I was close to taking the step of working as a medium myself when I learned that I was pregnant with Kasper. Shortly afterwards I was pregnant with Layla and we made the decision to move our burgeoning family down to Sussex.

Then followed three years of quietly setting up my reflexology and doula practice in my new abode and enjoying family life with two lively youngsters. As much as my spiritual life was important to me, I just didn't have the time or energy to maintain it. Plus, we were living in a small, relatively conservative village. I didn't dare tell anyone that I was a medium except for my neighbour and good friend, Em. I've never been one to worry about what others think of me but I felt anxious that my fellow villagers' perceptions of me might somehow reflect badly on our children and I so wanted to be accepted as part of a small community and enjoy all that this had to offer us as a family. And so, not for the first time, my "other life" took a back seat. For a while after Romy died it stayed off my radar and I shied away from stepping back in to what I had previously known so well as I tried to deal with my all-consuming grief, anger and disbelief at what had happened. At that point in my life if I had had a more conventional faith, I would have lost it. It turned out, though, that I couldn't stay away from Spirit. As much as I tried to distance myself, it started to draw me back quite persistently.

In early November of that year I found myself ensconced in Gerrie's London flat. I had asked her if she would give a sitting, wanting to do it professionally and pay for her time, but she point-blank refused to take my money and invited me to her flat to sit together and see what might come out of it. Gerrie is a very private person so it was a great honour to be invited into her personal space, and the information I received from her did not disappoint, as I knew it wouldn't.

Gerrie began by talking about Darius. For the record, I had not told her any information about the ending of his business partnership or the ensuing difficulties. Gerrie correctly pinpointed "an incident in September" that had really knocked him sideways, as she put it. She then said that she saw him getting on a plane for his work. This was something that was not happening at that point, but during a recent visit to the Spiritualist church the medium on the platform that evening had said exactly the same thing. Even more bizarrely, I had told Darius some time before this that I felt that he would be travelling internationally for his work – something that I knew would benefit him greatly even though he was reluctant to leave me and the children. He did, and still does, travel frequently for his work and enjoys the sense of freedom and stimulation it brings.

Gerrie then immediately connected with an image of Romy; significantly, *as she would have been at that time should she have lived.* This was immensely significant to me as during the two occasions I "saw" her it was always at the approximate age that she would have been; not at the age that I last saw and remembered her. Children change rapidly during their first two years, and on the second occasion I saw Romy in a vision, I hardly recognised her. It was a very strange feeling. Gerrie described Romy as being at the age where she was beginning to cut teeth and that she was being cared for by a number of people from both sides of our family, one of whom looked as if she had been a nurse during the war years. This corresponded exactly with the description given to us by Jan of the nurse with the starched white hat. I still couldn't place her, but wondered again whether it could be the woman I had seen during my facial when I saw Romy standing next to a woman of that description who was carrying a baby boy.

Gerrie mentioned my godmother who had played a significant role in our lives when we were younger and who had passed some years before. She told me that this godmother had given my mother a ring (this is correct – my mother had visited her during her last days when she had been given this ring as a gift). She described a tall, intellectual-looking man with Romy who spoke an ancient-sounding language. This could be either Darius's father, whom I never met, or another of his Persian family members who spoke Farsi. To my surprise, she then said that the house we had just viewed and agreed to put in an offer on was not the right house for us. She said that the next house we felt serious about would be "the one" and described in minute detail the position and aesthetics of the house we would go on to buy. Gerrie did know that we were planning a move but we had not seen that house at that point. This was in November 2014. She said that we would find the house in February, and according to my diary of that year we viewed it for the first time on 2nd February – just two days after I found out that I was pregnant with Macsen.

The final pieces of information she gave to me were small, but staggering in their significance to me. When I last visited Romy at the funeral director's I took several items with me. Most of these were known to Darius: one of my T-shirts (a part of me couldn't bear her going anywhere without something comforting with my scent on), some drawings done by the children and a letter I had written her. I asked for some time alone with her and it was then that I placed in her casket two additional items: one that I won't name here and one that I will. The point of both these items being unknown to anyone except myself was that I knew that at some point I would consult a medium and I wanted to have indisputable proof that they were receiving information from Romy's spirit. I told Darius of my plan but did not even share the identity of those two items with him. That way, if they ever came up in a reading, I would know for certain that Romy was communicating with me.

Gerrie started to describe a toy that Romy had with her. She said it was a small toy, an animal, she thought a rabbit. It was either pink or a soft pastel colour and it had particularly soft ears. This was what I had been waiting for. Layla is a big fan of soft toys and one of her particular favourites at that time was a small toy rabbit with very soft fur. This rabbit – called Flip Flop – went to bed with her each night and accompanied her everywhere. That Easter, when choosing gifts for the children I had picked out a matching toy rabbit for Romy – a smaller size than Layla's, pale lilac in colour and with the trademark soft ears. It was this that I had secretly placed with her as it held so much significance for me, and I also wanted her to continue to have that link with her sister. It was a wonderful moment to have that toy rabbit identified by Gerrie when nobody, not even Darius, had known it was in the casket with Romy.

Finally, Gerrie said that Romy would be sending me an actual gift at Christmas time. She said that this would take the form of a small, seemingly significant item that would find itself in my hands just before or on Christmas Day. She finished by saying that Romy's purpose, as she matures in the spirit world, is to work on the prevention of conflict. This came to represent great meaning to us both as we came to see the impact Romy had made on a number of areas of conflict in our own lives. She finished by telling me that my purpose is to tell grieving parents that their children are not lost.

As we half-heartedly prepared for Christmas a few weeks later I was searching our kitchen for a small, star-shaped cookie cutter. Layla and I have an annual tradition of making mince pies with a pastry star shape on top. I turned the whole kitchen upside down but could not find the cookie cutter. As we sat down to lunch on Christmas Day, Kasper pulled my cracker with me and out flew a star-shaped cookie cutter. The five-pointed star is a symbol I associate with Romy and I felt that this was the gift that Gerrie had told me would come to me. I had dreamed of continuing our mince pie tradition with both our daughters in the years to come, so Romy had been very much in my mind during that activity. It felt as if she were letting me know that she was with us, watching and helping in her own way with family Christmas preparations.

Later that same month I decided, on a whim, to attend a psychic fayre in Hove. I had only found out about it the day beforehand and as I mentioned it to Darius I found myself questioning the wisdom of going. However, this had happened to me before – a strange pull towards some kind of psychic event – and it always resulted in an inspirational sitting. I decided to trust my vibes and go along. As I wandered through the town hall in which the event was staged, I scanned the tables with resident psychics as I was so sure that I was meant to be seeing one of them. Unusually, they were all free and sitting ready to work but I just wasn't drawn to any of them. It was then that my eyes alighted on a table with a garish flashing angel positioned on it. The owner of the stall wasn't there. "Oh my goodness," I thought, "that's just the opposite of what would encourage me to have a sitting with that person!" I drew closer to the table. The appointment list was sitting there along with a note that said that the psychic was giving a demonstration of mediumship right then in the main hall. I reasoned that if this psychic had been asked to give a dem, she must be pretty good. I looked again at the list. There was one slot left. Impulsively, I wrote my name on it and waited.

I found Anne to be warm, kind and direct. She specifically told me not to give her any additional information during the half hour sitting and to answer simply with "yes", "no" or "I don't know". She went on to explain that "I don't know" wasn't good enough for her and that she would always seek to present the information in a way that I could understand. She kicked off by describing my grandfather in precise detail, followed, to my immense surprise, by my godmother – the same woman whom Gerrie had described to me just weeks previously. She then began to tell me that she could sense the presence of a recently passed spirit who had been very young. She asked me if I wished to continue and I said yes. Here is how our conversation went from that point:

"I have here a beautiful child, like an angel, with unbelievably blue eyes. There's something about her eyes. The colour is so intense and unusual, and I feel that people would have commented on those eyes and on her seeming old beyond her years (yes they had, often). This child is an old soul and only needed to return to earth this one last time as she needed to learn how to love and be loved. She communicated with others using her eyes, this is very significant." I was astonished at how much emphasis Anne placed on this point as I lost count of the amount of times in Romy's short time with us people had passed comment on her compelling cornflower blue eyes. The photographs we have of her are remarkable in their gaze and focus.

"I'm seeing that she doesn't need to come back as she is highly evolved and just needed to complete this last jigsaw piece of her purpose before returning home. Did she not have very much hair?" Okay, first "fail". Romy had absolutely loads of hair; everyone commented on it. I hadn't uttered a word in response when she corrected herself: "Oh no, hang on a minute, that's not it. She lost some hair – a lock of her hair was cut. I'm being shown an exaggerated image of a patch of missing hair. You have a lock of her hair in a locket and you're wearing it now." This was very impressive. I was wearing a gold locket given to me by Darius and containing Romy's photograph and the lock of hair we had cut, but prior to entering the venue I had already thought of hiding it. Being November, I was wearing a heavy coat and a scarf, with layers underneath, and I had carefully tucked the locket down inside my clothes and positioned the scarf over the top. I had even checked my reflection in the restroom before going upstairs to make sure that nothing would be visible as I felt sure that it would be a very obvious giveaway to a medium.

"She is thanking you. She says that you were there with her for every last step of the way. She says that there was no pain at her passing, just a little difficulty breathing (correct), before she fell asleep and didn't wake up (this would fit with my instinctive feeling that in some way Romy left us while we were still in the living room of our home, where she had lost consciousness). There was nothing anyone could have done and you both need to stop feeling such guilt. She says that your husband feels terribly guilty at not being able to protect her, and you. She is thanking you for a truly beautiful ceremony and for taking her flowers – you go every single week (true)."

Anne went on to describe a recent problem with Darius's wisdom tooth, refer to Layla's psychic ability and Kasper's high energy and sensitivity, all with succinct accuracy. She said that Romy often visits Darius in dreams, which was particularly startling as he had mentioned just weeks previously that he had dreamed about her. I was upset, asking why I didn't have dreams of her, so desperate was I to see, hear, or hold her, even in a virtual sense. Before I could ask Anne any questions about this she went on to say that Spirit does bring Romy to me in dreams but that I am not yet permitted to recall those dreams as it would not be beneficial to my healing. The wound was still too raw and I would wake missing her intensely. As it was, she said, after such visitations I wake feeling inexplicably sad and with a lack of energy. This was true; I had had several mornings like this on which I had woken with a terrible, gnawing feeling that I was missing something. I had assumed that this was just another part of the grief spectrum but on these particular days I found myself with a sadness that I just couldn't shake. As soon as Anne mentioned this, I felt reassured.

Suddenly, Anne asked me, "Are you planning another

baby?" I started to stutter something about it being a difficult question to answer. The truth was, I was starting to feel as if that was a possibility but Darius couldn't quite bring himself to think about it. I explained briefly that I wasn't sure and that my husband definitely didn't share my feelings at this point. Anne responded that maybe she had misinterpreted the information. However, several minutes later she revisited the topic: "Look I'm sorry, I don't usually give information like this but I'm being told categorically that there is another baby. Your family is not complete until this person joins you. And you'd better hurry up and prepare because they'll be arriving sooner than you think!" Within eight weeks of that sitting I was pregnant.

The last piece of information Anne gave me felt staggering. She described a large screen television in our living room which could be wall mounted but, she said, it wasn't – it was balanced on the top of a piece of dark wood furniture and had the ability to rotate around one hundred and eighty degrees. I marvelled at the specific nature of this description but couldn't understand why she was telling me this. "Have you seen this television move?" she asked me. I went to answer, "No," when something stopped me in my tracks. No, I had not *seen* the TV move, but on several mornings over the past two weeks I had come downstairs to find the screen tilted at a ridiculous angle. Annoyed, and thinking that Darius must have knocked it while plugging in one of his many electronic gadgets I sighed to myself as I moved it back into place, meaning to take it up with him. Or perhaps, I thought, Kasper was mucking about with the TV.

Anne was adamant. "Your daughter is moving the television screen. She has done it on more than one occasion and she is doing it to let you know that she's around you." In all the years I have undertaken psychic development myself and visited numerous mediums and psychics, I have to admit that this information was hard for me to swallow. I just didn't know what to do with it. It took me a couple of days after returning home to fully digest what Anne had told me and I held back from telling Darius about the baby and the TV as I just didn't know how he would take it. Finally, one evening I asked, "Have you been moving the TV screen when you plug your phone charger in? It's really annoying me." He gave me a funny look and replied, "No, I've noticed that that keeps happening and I thought it was you!" We both agreed that we had each independently noticed the unbalanced TV screen more than once as we came downstairs first thing in the morning and discussed whether or not it might have been the children. Despite the fact that this meant that they would have had to move and stand on a piece of furniture to reach it (they were then only four and five years old) and that they would have managed to creep downstairs on their own before 6am without waking us, we decided that it was possible. I came clean and described what Anne had told me and we spent a couple of hours discussing various scenarios. We agreed that we would try to find ways of asking Kasper and Layla whether they were moving or touching the television without asking leading questions but in the end there was no need because after that conversation *the TV never moved again*. I took this as the confirmation we needed. After all, if it had been an innocent occurrence, the chances of it happening again given its prior frequency were high. I like to think that Romy had made her point and stopped to further prove to us that it was indeed her doing.

She didn't stop at moving the TV screen either. We moved into our new home in Brighton in June 2015 and spent a frantic few months decorating and having work done to the house before I gave birth that October. I was particularly proud of the living room, which I had identified early on as a space that felt good for me to write in. I installed a desk next to our new wood burning stove and surrounded my work space with my favourite objects: crystals, inspirational quotes and photographs. After Macsen arrived I lovingly hung a photograph of each of our four children, vertically in order of descending age. It was almost three years later that these photographs were to catch my attention for more than the usual reasons. Over the course of several weeks in Spring 2018 I found myself glancing over at the pictures and on more than one occasion Romy's was somehow askance. As I righted it for the third time in as many weeks I found myself wondering how this could be happening. Were the children jumping up and down on their bedroom floors above and causing mini tremors? Was the hanging thread on the back of the frame loose? My main question, however, concerned the fact that Romy's was the only one of the four pictures to move in any way. Week after week it would end up on a slant while the two pictures above and one below remained resolutely straight. On the fourth or fifth occasion, I blurted out loud, "Romy, you're doing this aren't you? I know it's you." It suddenly seemed clear to me that, just in the same way as she had apparently caused our TV to move, Romy was succeeding in drawing my attention to her photograph. A week or two later I was attending a mediumship development course. Over three days I was privileged to sit with and learn from several experienced mediums. Away from my normal domestic existence it was like food for the soul and I soaked up the atmosphere and all the information like a sponge. I'd told myself that I was relaxed about receiving any kind of messages or information for myself: I'm a big believer in trusting that the right message will find its way to you if Spirit decide that it's important. Every evening one or two of the mediums would take to the platform to give a demonstration of their skills and by the end of the third such demonstration I felt my spirits drop a little as I realised that I had been waiting for some kind of message after all. Luckily I had booked myself in for a sitting on the final morning and as I got ready in my hotel room beforehand I sent out a thought to my grandmother Sylvia. "Please bring Romy," I mentally beseeched her. "I know she's okay but I'd love to hear that she's with you and being looked after. I miss her so much and I just need something from her." Two hours later, I was sitting opposite Craig, a young medium who had come to the event to give demonstrations and sittings. He had not taught any of the classes and I hadn't mixed with him socially at all. In fact, the only contact I'd had with him over the course of the entire weekend was a couple of polite hellos in passing. Craig began describing a woman who closely resembled my grandmother in both physical form and personality. "She heard your thoughts this morning as you got ready to come here and she's bringing a child with her, a little girl," Craig told me. "She wants you to know that this little girl is growing up in the spirit world and that she's being looked after by herself and other loved ones. She brings her to visit you often, sometimes while you sleep, and your grandmother knows that it's important for you to hear this today." These were very emotional words to hear and I couldn't help but let some tears flow as Craig described Romy to me, including her brilliant blue eyes. He then continued, "You have a photograph of her on your living room wall and it's been moving. Your daughter wants you to know that she's been making it go wonky to attract your attention; you know she can do this." This was amazing to hear. Once again, my gut feeling had been correct and to have this corroborated by a man who had never met me before was reassuring and filled me with joy. As before, once I had heard this information the picture never moved again.

In among these private sittings I attended my local Spiritualist church pretty much every Saturday evening for many months until Romy's first birthday – 26th March 2015 – when I was already pregnant with Macsen. I first went just weeks after she died and returned home in tears. I hadn't particularly connected with the medium on the platform giving the demonstration and had spent the whole evening shrinking further and further into my seat, wondering what on earth I was doing there. "I'm never setting foot in one of those places again!" I ranted at Darius when I got home later that night. "It was a massive mistake."

Imagine, then, his surprise when a mere two weeks later I blithely asked him, "Would you mind if I went out to the Spiritualist church this evening?" "What, you mean the one that you are never setting foot in ever again?" came his reply. Once again, I found myself en route to a place where Spiritualists gather, all the while asking myself what on earth I thought I was doing. I thought that I had left this part of my life behind me a long time ago. I drove myself there alone, in silence except for the one-sided conversation I was holding with Romy. "Romy," I said out loud to my empty car, "I said I wasn't coming back to this place but I know there's a reason why Spirit have called me back. I know in my heart that you're okay, but I'm still your mummy and I miss you desperately and I really just need to hear from you that you're okay. I need to hear it from you. That's all."

The medium giving the demonstration that night was a lively, vivacious woman, who explained that she receives information extremely fast and gives it just as quickly. She asked us not to be unnerved that she appeared to be barking out messages and assured us that she would be around to answer questions afterwards for those of us who needed to ask them. I sat at the back of the crowded hall, having once again checked and double-checked that my locket was well hidden underneath my clothes and the light scarf I had wound around my neck as I left the house. I knew with absolute certainty that she was going to give me a message, and I knew that I would be the third person she came to.

I was right on both counts. She fired a barrage of information at me from one or two relatives before saying that she saw a very young girl, a baby. She said, "You're wearing a locket around your neck with a lock of her hair and a photograph in it and you hold this locket and talk to her a lot." This was absolutely correct, down to the precise way that she was showing me I held it. Aside from this, information concerning Romy was scant and she was about to direct her beam on to the next person when she said, "I'm being told I must tell you something but that my choice of words is very, very important." I waited with bated breath, expecting some kind of lengthy eulogy from Spirit. Instead, she said, "They are really stressing that the way I tell you this is of the utmost importance and it's only two words. They're telling me to tell you, 'I'm okay.'"

I felt as if the breath had been knocked out of my body. If anybody out there can tell me how this woman – having never met me before and having had no way of overhearing what I'd asked my deceased daughter to tell me, out loud in my car, alone, just an hour previously – could have come up with those uncannily specific two words then I'm all ears. Despite my beliefs and my grief-stricken desperation to want to believe what she told me, still I have gone over it time and again, almost willing myself to find a way to discount it because it's almost too much to take in. I had asked Romy directly to tell me herself that she was okay. Through that medium, she told me, "I'm okay." And for those of you thinking that there's no way a four-month-old baby could have known, or used, words, please remember that once Romy passed to Spirit she was no longer a being in human baby form but a soul, returning from whence she came.

Prompt: Have you ever sought out communication with those who have passed? Have you experienced it for yourself, either in a dream or through a broad daylight experience which has stayed with you and which you cannot explain away, try as you might? Have you felt afraid by this experience or has it given you comfort and reassurance?

Chapter 13

Lestat, The Sentinel

What greater gift than the love of a cat.
– Charles Dickens

In any book about spiritual connection there should always be a place for animals as their love is so pure and they live alongside us both as our companions and our teachers. As I wrote this very chapter our beloved cat Lestat left us to go home to Spirit.

We rehomed Lestat from a Cats Protection rescue centre near us in Sussex and from the very beginning it was clear that he had chosen us. Now, almost exactly five years later, I think I know why. I believe that Lestat and Romy came as a pair and that he somehow deliberately preceded her in joining our family and left only once he saw that I was on my path back to my purpose and my life.

One Saturday, Darius suggested taking the children, then aged three and five, to the local Cats Protection rehoming centre "to have a look round". As my sister incredulously remarked afterwards, asking me – a lifelong animal lover and ex-employee of Battersea Dogs & Cats Home – to visit an animal rescue centre and expecting to return home without an animal was nothing short of ludicrous. Nevertheless, off we went.

Once there, Layla was sleeping in the car so I took Kasper inside. Transfixed by the very first pen we encountered, Kasper exclaimed, "Mama, look at that cat!" I looked at where he was pointing. I couldn't see anything. I peered closer. Inside a furry igloo bed were glowing two huge yellow-green eyes. Surrounding the eyes was a little triangular black face and two pointy ears. We had met Lestat. I felt magnetically drawn to him and heard myself say impulsively, "Let's ask Daddy if we can get him." By the time Darius arrived inside with Layla we had toured the remaining area and seen some truly beautiful cats but we kept returning to the pen containing Lestat. Noticing my streaming eyes, Darius sympathetically asked whether being in the centre had triggered my cat allergy (something that started during childhood and which all but disappeared after four years of working at Battersea). "No!" I wailed. "I'm crying because I can't believe all these cats don't have homes, and we have to get one. This one!"

My slightly bemused husband asked a member of staff to open Lestat's pen so we could meet him and we then proceeded to have a mini domestic dispute in front of the embarrassed young rehomer. I was adamant that we were taking this cat home. Darius quite reasonably countered that he was nine years old, that he came from a home with twenty-two other cats so he might not be very sociable with humans (not great for the kids, or for the cat), we would risk losing him a few short years after having him, and so on. He finished lamely with, "And we didn't come here to get a cat." In the end he put his foot down and said that we were going to go home and discuss it in a civilised manner and if, when we had finished this discussion and reached an agreement, the cat were still available, then he would *consider* it. I'm not ashamed to admit that I cried all the way home and threw a childish tantrum about the whole episode. Once home I decided not to mention it further, either to Darius or the children, but my heart was heavy and I was obsessing over this cat who I was absolutely certain was supposed to be with our family.

The next morning was Sunday. I woke up thinking about Lestat but again, decided not to mention it that day as I didn't want to disappoint the children, who were still blissfully unaware that a cat could be part of our future. At around 6am Kasper came into our bedroom, got into bed between us, turned to Darius and said, "Daddy, are we going to get the cat today?" Of course, Darius immediately looked accusingly at me as if I had engineered an emotional blackmail scenario, but I assured him indignantly and truthfully that I hadn't said a word. Kasper had obviously also woken up thinking about Lestat; or had he somehow tapped in to my mind? If he had, it wouldn't be the first time. I have to say that, although Layla is the most obviously psychic of my children, I have often thought that my highly sensitive eldest boy has an uncanny knack of tuning in to my thoughts and feelings and will somehow find a way to express them when I can't, or have decided not to.

Darius asked Kasper what he meant. He reiterated, "Daddy, are we going to the cat centre again to get that cat, the black one?" Darius gently replied that no, we were not planning a trip to the cat centre today and that we would probably get a cat, but that we needed to discuss it properly first and to decide together as a family what we would do. "But, Daddy," he beseeched, "that poor cat doesn't have a home and he needs to live with us." That did it. Within five minutes Darius was growling at me, "Okay, call and ask if we can go in today." A week later, Lestat was ours. Or more accurately, to which any cat owner will attest, we were his.

Lestat was the name given to him by the rehoming centre, presumably because he was a black cat as Lestat is the name of the main character in Anne Rice's novel, *Interview with the Vampire*. We tried all sorts of alternative naming games with the children. However, Kasper was insistent that he should remain Lestat the Cat, and it always amused me to hear my six foot three ex-rower of a husband calling him in from the garden! For his first few weeks with us the poor thing wouldn't come out from underneath the sofa in our conservatory. I spent hours crawling around on the floor with bowls of fresh chicken, smelly tuna fish and various cat treats to no avail. He would creep out and eat when we weren't around. As the weeks passed, I tried not to feel disappointed that we seemed to have ended up with a family pet that showed no signs of wishing to integrate with us.

However, little by little he began to come out of his shell and climb up on top of the sofa for some attention. After a while he seemed to realise that he was the sole feline in a house full of humans who loved him, and came to enjoy the attention and love – albeit always on his own terms. Within months, it was his nightly habit to curl himself around Darius's shoulders for the evening while we sat on the sofa – quite a turnaround for a previous "pack member" not accustomed to human attention. Kasper, always a painfully early riser in the mornings, formed a particularly strong bond with him and surprised us all with his patience and calmness around our new pet.

By the June of that year I was pregnant with Romy and it was Lestat who let me know. As a reflexologist working with fertility and pregnancy I had seen this phenomena before when working with clients in their own homes who had cats. I recall giving reflexology to a regular client who was hoping to become pregnant. The cat of the house would usually greet me as I arrived and then either show immense interest in the reflexology session by weaving around my legs as I worked, or sit close by in the room. I have always thought that animals sense the shift in energy in the room and feel drawn to the calm created when a person is receiving healing of any sort. During the session, the cat jumped on to its owner, settled on to her midriff and stayed there despite attempts to move it. I thought to myself, "Surely she must be pregnant and the cat knows it." Of course, it would not have been professional to announce this so I kept quiet but I received a phone call shortly afterwards from an ecstatic client saying that she had just found out she was pregnant. This happened, not just once, but on two occasions with two separate clients and their cats. Lestat did this with a client in our home once too. Usually aloof with unknown visiting humans, he came right up to this lady and as she reclined on my reflexology chair he insisted on jumping on to her lap, settled on to her midriff and would not budge. Luckily, she liked cats, and wouldn't you know it, a few days later she called to tell me that she was pregnant.

And so it was with my own pregnancy. Despite having a kind of knowing in the back of my mind, I couldn't bring myself to acknowledge that I might in fact be pregnant for the third time as I wasn't sure I could cope with the disappointment if my feeling was wrong. A few weeks after we returned from Spain I couldn't bear the suspense any longer and decided to put myself out of my misery and move forwards one way or another. I bought a pregnancy test. As always, the wait for the little blue line seemed to go on forever, and eventually, after scrutinising it for some time, I reluctantly had to admit to myself that it was negative. I felt numb. All my instincts had told me that I would be having another baby. I could *feel* her presence, literally hanging around in the ether. I began to think that perhaps I was going mad. I went downstairs to make a cup of tea and sit for a moment with my thoughts. Unusually, Lestat came running from his spot in the warm conservatory and jumped on to my lap without warning. I wondered if perhaps he could sense my sadness in some way and was trying to help. He was, however, a real creature of habit and would never deign to join us, his humans, for "lap time" until after the children had gone to bed. He never deviated from this practice. Then his behaviour became even more unusual. He started to circle round and round on my lap and couldn't settle. I put him down on the floor. He jumped back up, straight on to my lap. I lay back a little on the sofa and he made a beeline for my abdomen and immediately lay down on it. I had a sudden flashback to my client whom he had greeted in the same way. At the same time I heard a voice in my "inner ear" announce, "Look at the test again." I raced upstairs and dredged the pregnancy test stick out of the bin. It was a bright sunny day in early July. I looked at the results window. Still blank. I stood next to the bathroom window, held it in the light and stared. I could hardly believe my eyes: the faintest of blue lines was showing against the white. Two more tests confirmed that I was in fact pregnant.

We noticed Lestat's behaviour again at Romy's birth. Lestat was also around when Macsen was born and his behaviour at the two births couldn't have been more different. Bear in mind that this was a cat who was wary of new people and situations; reticent and nervous. Romy's birth began one evening as Darius and I were eating dinner. Lestat was wound round Darius's neck as usual and I was eating spaghetti. I suddenly felt nauseous, and before I knew it, contractions were at full pelt. While Darius ran around calling midwives and literally getting towels and hot water ready, Lestat was nowhere to be seen. However, as events intensified he appeared from nowhere, started climbing about on the sofa I was crouched over and would not get out of the way. Luckily, our midwife Lisa was a cat lover and not too phased by his behaviour but suggested that it might be better if we moved him into the conservatory. Darius did this and for the next half an hour he caterwauled constantly, threw himself against the door and desperately tried everything he could to get back by my side. Knowing him as we did as such an aloof and reserved creature, this was truly extraordinary behaviour. The minute Romy was safely in my arms, we opened the conservatory door and out flew Lestat. He ran straight to the sofa (on which I was now sitting) and planted himself right next to me, sitting bolt upright, guarding me like an upright version of an Egyptian sphinx. In contrast, when Macsen was born, he just absented himself. No meowing, no scrabbling at the door. He was nowhere to be seen and in fact I recall sitting on the sofa with a newly born Macsen asking Darius if he had seen the cat anywhere when, as if by magic, in he strolled. Like before, he jumped up next to me, sniffed the new arrival but then he jumped down and went off to one of his usual curling-up spots.

There could be a number of reasons why these two situations were so different. Different house, different environment, different time of day. Lestat was over a year older and his health had suffered a slight decline; maybe he wasn't feeling well. I'd go with any of these suggestions but I know in my heart that they are not true. As utterly crazy as this may sound, I believe that somehow Lestat and Romy were meant to come together. His intense behaviour at her birth seems somehow like a desire to make good on a contract to accompany and protect her. I refer to him in this chapter title as a "sentinel": *"a person or thing that watches or stands as if watching"*. This is always how his presence felt to me.

His departure came two and a half years after hers, and I believe that this was perfectly timed. It was only when I started to climb out of the black hole of my grief and look forwards that Lestat's health began to deteriorate. We hadn't been aware of any illness when we rehomed him but he was at least ten years of age so it was fairly likely that he would start to slow down as time went on. However, we weren't prepared for how sudden his demise would be. It was as if my strength grew as his lessened and it makes me feel a little sad to think of this, but I also like to think that he volunteered himself as my protector. And what a job he did. In the worst days of my grief I would drop the children at school, come home and secrete myself in the house with him, crying for hours. If I felt terrible, he would often seek me out and curl up on my lap. His antics made the children laugh and I often pretended to be his "voice", which greatly amused Kasper in particular.

Two days after Lestat left us, I found myself feeling bereft, plunged back into the awful darkness that enveloped me after Romy died. I know it sounds silly and possibly disrespectful to compare our daughter's death to that of our cat's, but I can only say that I was dismayed to find myself experiencing echoes of the grief I felt just over two years previously. In the early days after Romy's death, a combination of grief and primal self-preservation caused me to operate on a purely functional level, all emotions in shutdown: making the beds, cooking lunch, shopping, all the while feeling a restlessness and a gaping hole in my daily life. For some of us, grief lies like a heavy stone in the heart: not big enough to overshadow anything and not small enough to ignore.

Similarly, in the first few days without our beloved cat we all felt echoes of some of these feelings. I kept imagining that I could see him in his habitual spots: on the radiator, snuggled inside the one blanket we always tried to keep cat-free, in the airing cupboard perched on top of a pile of freshly washed towels. There's the thing though; I was imagining it. I wondered, how I could possibly call myself any kind of medium or psychic? I couldn't even connect with my beloved pet.

Several days after Lestat left us I was putting Layla to bed and she revealed to me a dream she'd had the night after he died. We'd talked a little bit about the spirit world, what I believed and where I thought Lestat was – a reiteration of some of the topics that had come up after her periods of interrupted nights and in the months following Romy's death. So one could easily come up with an explanation that says that Layla and her fertile imagination had somehow mixed together everything we'd talked about to construct this dream. But I think I know better. In her dream, according to Layla, "… Lestat was running around like a little kitten in the spirit world and Romy was throwing a ball for him." "Wow," I replied, trying to hide my excitement and being conscious not to lead her anywhere with my comments or questions. "What else did you see in your dream?"

"Lots of people were there as well."

"Really, sweetie? Who?"

"Great-Aunt Jeannette, Grandpa Noory and some other people I didn't know."

"Oh okay. That sounds like a lovely dream."

"It was, Mummy. We all watched Romy and Lestat playing and then we all went and sat down under a huge tree with some blankets and we all snugged up together (our family term for snuggling up with blankets) and ate some lovely food, like a picnic."

I was amazed at what Layla had told me and wondered whether the other people she mentioned could have been family members she didn't recognise or even spirit guides or helpers. I could tell that she was nearly asleep so I restrained myself from asking her any more questions. Incredibly, as if she were reading my mind, she gave one more comment just before her eyes closed. "Mummy, do you know how I knew it was the spirit world?" "No, darling, I don't. How could you tell?" The answer was stunningly simple but also incredibly revealing to me. "The grass was so green – it was the greenest grass you've ever seen."

Two parts of Layla's description jumped out at me: the mention of the huge tree and also the green grass. In two visions I had months after Romy passed – neither of which I have ever shared with her in any way – these were very significant details. In the first, I was in a meadow and the grass was an achingly verdant shade of green. I was sitting underneath the spreading branches of a huge oak tree when Romy came to me. In the second vision, I saw her standing underneath a similar tree with a woman who I recognised from my work as a reflexologist and healer years before and a tiny baby who I knew was the baby I had just found out I was expecting.

Coincidence? I personally don't believe there is any such thing. Imagination? Possibly; although I support the theory that there is nothing so dangerous to human spiritual progression than the term "imagination". A six-year-old girl cobbling together things she has overheard to form some kind of spiritual experience with which to impress her mother? Again, possible. Let's face it, a sceptic will always find a way to discredit anything that they find to be uncomfortable or downright unbelievable. Maybe they are right – I'm open to that possibility too. However, I'm a creature of instinct and I happen to trust my instincts, and those of my children. I believe that my daughter was given a glimpse into life on the other side and I find it particularly apt that Lestat appears to have chosen Layla to communicate with. She was the one person in our family who always retained some kind of indifference towards him. How typical of a cat to gravitate towards that indifference.

Around ten days after Lestat's departure I started to ask Darius about the possibility of getting another cat. This was a difficult conversation as we were both in different places emotionally. Poor Darius had had to drive Lestat to the out-of-hours vet several miles from our home at 11pm on a cold Sunday night in January and he had found the whole experience terribly upsetting. His feeling, not unreasonably, was that our much-loved cat had hardly been gone ten minutes and I was already talking about a replacement. I, on the other hand, felt completely bereft without a cat in the house. I missed my old friend desperately and it was I who was spending hours in the house without his quiet companionship. I was listening to the children reminiscing about what he did at various points in the day before crying inconsolably as the reality of the situation reared its head and they remembered that he was gone. For the children, for our family and for myself I wanted to feel the familiar presence of four paws and a purr in the house again. It felt horribly incomplete without them. We attempted a few conversations about getting a new feline companion but they always seemed to disintegrate into bickering: over when we could get a cat, whether it was one cat or two, cats or kittens, rescue or pedigree. I felt Darius's resolve strengthening and decided to leave well alone for a week or two while we all calmed down.

Then one night, deep in sleep, I was woken by a loud purring in my right ear; as if a cat was on the pillow just above my head. We had never allowed Lestat into our bedroom in our Brighton home, mainly due to the fact that Macsen was born shortly after we moved there and we were always concerned about the cat and the baby sharing bed space. Obviously, at this point in time we did not own a cat but I did not remember this in my confused, half-asleep state. I sat up with a start, trying to rouse Darius by saying, "Quick, the cat's got into the bedroom. Can you get him out?" Darius collected himself for a minute before saying, "Ali, we don't have a cat." And that was it: the confirmation I had so wanted that my dear friend was safe and well in the spirit world. He had chosen to visit me to let me know this, and just to make his point he had taken the opportunity to make the forbidden leap on to the marital bed (my pillow, no less!) and purr loudly in my ear.

A week or two later everything had settled and we were the proud owners of a stunningly beautiful two-year-old ginger tom called Pika, who fits right in to our family. The children delight in his exceptional talents, which include sitting on command and giving "high fives" with one or both paws. Kasper refers to him as a "dat": his own terminology for a cat who thinks he's a dog. A few months later Pika was joined by a diminutive black cat by the name of Bagheera, who the children immediately decided was to be known as Baggy. As much as we adored Pika, we all felt a black cat shaped hole in our family and so we made another trip to Cats Protection and returned with Baggy, a two-year-old whose date of birth was given as 17th July 2014: the day that Romy began her journey home. After a few weeks of hissing and growling the two cats formed a lovely bond and are now an amusing double act, always seeking new ways to help themselves to food from the kitchen while our backs are turned. Darius and I often wonder how we managed to become outnumbered by children and animals. Nothing in our family life is run-of-the-mill.

Prompt: If you have a pet or pets, do you ever sense that they have somehow picked up on your feelings? Have they appeared in your life at an apparently coincidental or opportune time? If a beloved pet has died, have you ever seen them afterwards in one of their favourite spots or in a dream?

Chapter 14

No Coming, No Going

No coming, no going,
No after, no before
I hold you close to me, I release you to be so free
Because I am in you and you are in me.
– Thich Nhat Hanh (Courtesy of Plum Village)

It bothered me greatly that it took several weeks following Romy's burial to place a plaque at her resting place in the woodland burial ground we had chosen. Darius and I spent hours searching through inspirational quotes and fragments from poems and songs but nothing quite seemed to speak to us in the way that we thought it should. In the end, of course, the right words found us. One sunny afternoon we sat with our children at their school, joining in with chants and songs led by visiting Buddhist monks and nuns. The small independent school we moved our children to just after Romy died is heavily influenced by Buddhist ethos. We had visited it with Romy the month before she passed and were already making frantic calculations to figure out whether we could afford to place all three of our children there. After she died we assumed we would need to put those plans on hold as our family had experienced too much upheaval already, but strangely, it was Kasper and Layla who drove the move. One afternoon in the garden, Kasper suddenly asked us whether he would be going to a new school in September. As far as I recall, we had been careful not to discuss any such plans in front of the children at any time until we were ready to ask for their input. Once again, Kasper surprised us with his apparent intuitive ability to know what was afoot. As a result, they began at the Dharma Primary School in September of 2014 and we have never regretted our decision.

The school community holds regular gatherings, or *pujas*, at which a selection of songs is sung. On that sunny September afternoon, the visiting monks suggested singing *No Coming, No Going* as they were about to depart for home – their meditation centre in France, also the residence of the respected Buddhist monk and peace activist Thich Nhat Hanh. The melody was hauntingly beautiful and extremely moving as they repeated the refrain,

No coming, no going,
No after, no before
I hold you close to me, I release you to be so free
Because I am in you and you are in me.

Darius and I looked at each other and we knew that these were the precise words we wanted for Romy's plaque. It sums up perfectly how I feel about death and dying. Death is indeed never a true separation. We may miss the physical presence of our loved ones in Spirit but we are never separate: from each other or from Spirit; our source. I love the idea that we may hold a loved one close to us – so close, in fact, that they are inside us, in our heart and mind – but that we may also rejoice in their soul's freedom. This is not about possession or ownership because this is not possible between two people. As Rumi's famous poem reminds us, "Our children are not our children." However, if we consider the idea that we are all inextricably blended at source, then we will never be separated from each other, even by death. Not only am I in Romy and she in me because we are mother and child, but our essence is one and the same because we all, in the end, belong to the same source regardless of what religion we practise, what faith we hold and what names we assign to our beliefs.

I have always held myself to be a spiritual person but only after the "death" of my daughter did I begin to live my beliefs more fully. I can attribute a big part of this shift to my understanding that we can never be separated from our loved ones, even by death. Our society places much emphasis on the physical absence of our departed loved ones but I believe that if we choose to use our natural abilities to foster a connection with them, then we will never feel bereft. I can honestly say that these ideals helped me to process my grief and to move forward with a purposeful life in ways I could never have imagined had I remained focused on my unwanted "separation" from my child. It could easily have consumed my life. Instead I feel as if I have been reborn as a better version of myself, and this is Romy's legacy. I see that I have been afforded an opportunity to help others who live with the same unbearable pain as I have known; not by persuading them to believe the same things as I do, but perhaps simply by opening their minds to the possibility that their loved one may still be living unseen alongside them. Throughout my life, and in particular while writing this book, I have conducted many hours of reading and research on the subject of the afterlife and spirit communication. Despite apparently widespread scepticism, I have been continually amazed at how many individuals from all walks of life, with varying forms of spiritual and religious practice or, in some cases, none, have all had some kind of brush with Spirit; something they cannot explain, usually linked to the memory of a loved one who has passed. Everyone has a story to tell, but many are too afraid of ridicule to share them.

I'll give you an example. Recently, I participated in a photo shoot for a well-known national daily newspaper. I had been asked by my friend Theresa Cheung and her co-author, medium Claire Broad, if I would give an interview to help promote their latest book, *Answers from Heaven*. When I arrived at the newspaper office's photographic studio for the shoot I felt nervous and defensive. I knew that the team assigned to me would be aware of the nature of our story and was prepared for what I thought of as typical journalistic scepticism about my beliefs and abilities. I braced myself to defend both to a bunch of sneering "non-believers". By the time I left two hours later, the makeup artist had spent an hour telling me about various signs she had received from her dead grandmother, one of the two photographers had sidled up to me and told me how fascinated she was by the world of mediumship and the second photographer whispered to me that she was "a believer" and then hit me with the bombshell that she had herself had a near death experience! I spent most of the shoot suggesting various books they might be interested in. Proof that even in the most unlikely situations people will admit that they have experienced something of "The Other". Usually I find that they are desperate to talk about it to someone who won't laugh at them. I don't profess to know it all but I am always struck by how grateful people are to have the opportunity to share their experiences with Spirit and how they seek reassurance that their loved one is in fact still beside them.

One of the major reasons I held back from taking the plunge into professional mediumship was fear of derision. Throughout history, people have been subjected to ridicule and persecution for daring to speak publicly about their spiritual beliefs; in particular if those beliefs have been regarded as outside the norm, or more conventional religious practices. From Mahatma Gandhi to former UK sports commentator turned spiritual practitioner David Icke, there are many individuals who have found themselves picked on for sharing their particular experiences of enlightenment. I often wonder why we do this to each other. As humans seeking answers about our existence I wonder why we don't all embrace each other's beliefs. It is human nature to wish to identify with a group and I may call myself a Spiritualist but I have a healthy curiosity, not to mention respect, for all religions and spiritual practices as long as they do not harm anyone. In my younger years I would declare myself as being against organised religion but as I've grown older I have met many wonderful, kind and generous people who practise many different religions and my life has been the better for knowing them. Despite knowing for most of my life that my abilities to connect with the spirit world can help others, I shied away from using my ability – until recently. I can only say very simply that if you have grieved for a child then very little in life holds any fear after that. These days, the prospect of ridicule holds very little fear as I know that no bad feeling in the world can come close to how I felt after I watched my daughter leave this life. I can state with confidence that I have no interest in "converting" anyone to what I believe – only in sharing it to help as much as I can. If my help is not wanted, then that's fine. If you do not believe what I believe, I respect your views and trust that we can still be friends. One of my dearest friends, Helen, regards most of what I believe and practise with considerable suspicion but we still enjoy a close friendship, full of love and respect. It is entirely possible for humans to live alongside each other with differing beliefs and practices and it is only fear that prevents us from doing so. Learning to live together in harmony is one of the greatest tests of human existence.

I am often asked whether I regularly connect with Romy in the spirit world. I have described some of the experiences I have had in this book, but no, I don't have unlimited, or even regular, communication with my daughter or any other departed spirits. It just doesn't work that way. As far as I'm aware, most mediums are unable to connect with specific loved ones during a sitting or demonstration – we are, quite literally, the "medium" through which those in spirit choose to communicate with their loved ones here on earth. It takes an inordinate amount of energy for some spirits to get through to us and we will always hear from the right person at the right time – regardless as to whether we or our sitter have asked for somebody else.

Sometimes there are very good reasons why our loved ones

hold back from communicating with us. For instance, I can easily imagine a situation in which I could have become obsessed with speaking to Romy to the point that my surviving children may have been missing out on my attention. I visited several mediums in the first two years after Romy passed and it was Anne, the lady who I spoke to at random at the psychic fayre, who told me categorically that I would not be hearing from Romy for a while. It was as if she had given Anne spectacular information to enable me enough understanding to move forward with my life in a healthy way, and then she had bowed out for a while to let me get on with living it. At that point, if I had been dreaming about her, seeing her in visions or receiving any kind of signs from her spiritually it would only have served to deepen my grief and make me miss her more. As much as I believe we are forever connected, the physical reality is that Romy is not here, I have three other children who need me and I need to carry on living my life on this earth without constantly wishing I were with her instead.

As Anne told me, "You won't be seeing her for a while now. You both have things to be getting on with," I knew instantly what she meant. I had a baby to create and nurture, two older children who needed my attention and love, a book to write, a house move to engineer and a whole new purpose to embrace. The time to move forwards had come. I also had a feeling that in several years from then I would myself be working as a medium and that Romy would, in some way, be helping me. This has yet to come to pass but I feel that in the year that Romy would have turned seven – 2021 – she will appear from time to time to help me in my mediumship work. Time will tell. In the meantime, I feel confident enough in my own special connection with Romy not to repeatedly visit mediums for contact with her.

She does still give me occasional messages, usually just when I am least expecting them. At Christmas 2016 Layla and I were chatting in her room. I noticed a music CD lying on the floor and began to gently chastise her about leaving fragile items like this lying around. As we talked, I picked it up and placed it on the bookshelf at the other end of the room. Layla was absolutely adamant that she hadn't left the CD on the floor and was getting quite animated about telling me so. We were both looking in the direction of the bookshelf and just as she uttered, "Mummy, I'm telling you, it wasn't me!" the disc flew off the shelf, moved about half a metre through the air and landed at our feet. Layla and I looked at each other, speechless. All I could think of to say was, "Layla, did you see that?" She replied quietly, "Yes, Mummy. I told you it wasn't me." Neither of us uttered another word on the subject but I couldn't help thinking that her sister had just made her presence known to us.

Shortly after this I returned to the Harry Edwards Healing Sanctuary – truly such a sanctuary to me – to write and have a healing session. Darius's mother Suzanne was visiting and for the first time I felt able to leave Macsen (then just a year old) for the day to take some much-needed time to focus on this book, and myself. This extraordinary place has always held a special place in my heart; as a healer, I found it impossible not to be affected by its energy and calm. On a personal level, having visited it with Darius just ten days after Romy passed, its healing properties have that little bit more meaning for me as it was there that I first experienced the vision of Romy with my paternal grandparents. I admit that when I returned a little part of me was hopeful that I might get to meet her again. As I relaxed on the couch and let the healing energy wash over me I struggled to stay awake. With a small child still sharing our bed, two older children to organise, a house to run and a book to write I was always tired and opportunities to rest seemed non-existent. I fought sleep for as long as I could, so desperate was I to see whether I would "see" Romy. I wanted to be as aware as possible if it did happen.

Before I knew it, I was aware of a tall man standing beside

me and my cheek brushed against some familiar fabric. It was the rough, warm fabric of a man's winter overcoat and I immediately recognised Darius's father, Noory, wearing a long black overcoat that he had often worn in life and that Darius had had in his possession when I first met him. I was surprised. I never knew Noory in this life as he died at least four years before Darius and I met, but I have had several encounters with him in Spirit. I feel in a way as if I do know him very well; on more than one occasion I have felt a strong sense of his personality and humour, and over the years I have been able to relay to Darius information relating to him that I know was previously unknown to me. Nevertheless, I was surprised to feel his presence on that day. I touched his arm in greeting and he gave me a warm hug. Then he drew my attention downwards and I saw that with him was a little girl. She couldn't have been more than two or three years old, she had dark hair and unmistakeable blue eyes: it was Romy.

What was interesting about this encounter for me was that this child did not look as I would have expected Romy to look. Once again, she appeared at the age she would have been had she lived. Her hair was worn in a style that somehow felt alien to me – I didn't think I would have styled her hair like that myself. I also recall that her clothes appeared a little old fashioned. Despite this, however, I knew without a shadow of a doubt that she was my daughter. I bent down to hug her and was instantly flooded with emotion. I couldn't contain it at all and began to cry on the healing couch. I can't describe how good it felt to hold my child but my joy was tinged with dread at having to let her go again. Although emotional, it had felt like a privilege to be given a window of access to Romy and immensely reassuring to know that she was being looked after by her grandfather as well as by her great-grandparents.

As I moved into this new phase of my life my grandmother Sylvia began to reappear more frequently, which seemed entirely appropriate. I began to sense her presence by my side in the kitchen as I cooked, just as I used to when she first passed. As I began writing this book I felt myself suffused by her fiery energy and drive. We always had that in common and used to joke that it was to do with our Aries birthdays, just one day apart: once either of us undertook a project we went at it with overpowering force and passion, and kept going until it was finished. After I submitted my book proposal to a publishing competition, heard that I had been unsuccessful and teetered on the brink of giving up it was my grandmother who came to me during a sitting and told me in no uncertain terms to "get myself out there". I followed this advice and got my book proposal out there. Within weeks, I had signed a publishing contract.

The more I pondered my future and worried what was to become of me, the more I surrendered to Spirit and the more messages and communications I seemed to receive. My maternal grandmother, Eleanor, seemed to make her presence known from time to time whenever I felt that I couldn't juggle family life with any kind of career. This was significant to me as she was a highly intelligent woman who lacked opportunity simply due to the times she lived in. During her life she would always stress to me the importance of going as far as possible with education, with reading and acquiring knowledge and of making the most of opportunities; family or not. I began to chat away to Spirit regularly just as I had as a child, just quietly in my head, but the main message I had for them was always, "I'm ready. We had a deal: I said I would do your work. Send it!"

Midway through writing this book I found the confidence to venture along to a local psychic development circle. It took months of looking up different circles before Spirit lead me to Dorothy Young, who exhibited extreme patience as I emailed her back and forth for weeks, asking questions and dithering about making a commitment to attend. Of course, I told her about Romy and my previous development work and Dorothy simply listened and told me I would be welcomed whenever I was ready to come. The clever woman obviously knew that Spirit would decide when I was ready to come, and I believe that they did. I walked in to a small group of kind, welcoming faces and for the first time in over three years, I did not feel the need to immediately tell everyone present about Romy. I felt that this would come when it was ready – or, seeing as these were all developing mediums like me, they would already know! I couldn't help laughing at myself a little as the big fear I held of returning to development circle involved my absolute terror of public demonstrations of mediumship. Strangely for someone who once begged her parents to let her apply for the Royal Academy of Dramatic Art and spent years fantasising about becoming an actress, my one experience of platform demonstration, as Gerrie's student, went well but I swore that I would never do it again. It's one thing learning lines or adopting a persona and then getting up on a stage in front of others, but giving a public demonstration of mediumship is another thing entirely. Not only do you have to rely upon Spirit turning up, you then have to sift through all the spirit communicators and match them with the right recipient among the audience. Even worse, you can't even hide behind a persona as you do this (although perhaps some mediums might) – you have to be yourself. This was clearly a lesson in trust for me, and as the weeks unfolded I grew to love my new group and even to begin to enjoy the mini demonstrations we did for each other on the tiny platform inside the sacred space where we met.

It was during the first of these demonstrations that Xian, my spirit guide, chose to make himself known to me. It was only the second group meeting I had attended and I had been thoroughly enjoying the discussions and group work we had been undertaking. Towards the end of our session, Dorothy spontaneously announced that we would be doing a brief practice of platform work. I froze in my seat. "We have a lovely platform here; let's use it!" she exclaimed in her enthusiastic way. "This is what we're all here to do – let's get to work!"

Usually pretty gung-ho in these situations, my fear got the better of me and I hung back, sitting through each of my fellow group members' impressive connections with Spirit until it unavoidably came to my turn. Praying that the clock would be on my side and that Dorothy would cut me short before I had a chance to make a total fool of myself, I made a quiet prayer to Spirit to please, please, send me some kind of connection – anything. As I stood on the platform, I tried to quiet my mind and focus but nothing was coming. All I could see was the image of a Chinese man in an ornate red brocade costume. I kept trying to brush it to one side so I could properly connect with somebody's deceased granny, father or friend, but try as I might, I just couldn't get this man out of my vision. I began to realise that I had seen him before. When I was doing my healer training in 2009 I would see him on my inner screen when I was performing healing and he would often tell me – using words I could hear, visions or symbols – where the root of the patient's health issue was. I never told anybody about him because in all honesty I wasn't really sure what I was dealing with, and there are strict rules regarding what you can tell a patient if you happen to receive psychic or mediumistic knowledge during a healing (absolutely nothing). During one of my last circle meetings with Gerrie she guided us through a meditation to meet one of our spirit guides and I saw this gentleman again.

As I stood on the platform politely trying to shift the Chinese gentleman to one side, I heard myself telling the group that it had been a very long time since I had done any sort of platform work, that I was crippled with nerves and that it was probably best that I just started talking to see what might come out. I'm not entirely sure what I said next, but when I had finished, everyone was nodding sagely and thanking me for the wisdom I had given. I felt that it had come from this man, and before I knew it, I was describing him and acknowledging him as my spirit guide. In my mind, I spoke to him for the first time. "What's your name?" I asked. "Now I've told everyone you're my spirit guide. Everyone's spirit guide seems to give a name so please can you tell me yours?" Straight away, I received the sound, "Shi-en," and my hands began to make strange shapes in the air. As they did this I received an image of the ancient art of Chinese calligraphy and I felt that I was being given Chinese characters which spelled out this man's name. I then saw, in Western script, the letters X, I, A and N accompanied by the same voice repeating, "Shi-en." Hardly daring to believe my own words, I told the group that my spirit guide was a Mandarin gentleman named Xian, and then it went quiet.

Several days later at home I found myself thinking over the events of that night and once again wondering whether I should trust the information I had received. What on earth was I thinking, I asked myself. It was probably all a figment of my imagination and I had conjured up a Chinese man called Xian because I was so nervous at the prospect of platform mediumship. I had probably heard the name in a film or television programme and my mind had come up with it at that moment. I was cooking dinner at the time and decided I would quickly do some Internet research on the name. I typed "Pronunciation of the name Xian" into my phone. It came up with something that sounded like *Zy-an*; nothing at all like the pronunciation I had been given. It was almost a relief. Okay, so I was right. There is no such name, pronounced in that way. I must have imagined it. Just as I was straining the vegetables, I heard the male voice again, clear as day. Rather wearily, as if speaking to a very small child, he said, "No. It is Mandarin. Check again." I typed in, "Pronunciation of Xian in Mandarin." It responded with *Shi-en*. I dropped the pan I was holding. Something then made me look up the meaning of the name and this is what I found:

Xian... is a Chinese word for an enlightened person, trans-
latable in English as: "spiritually... immortal; transcendent;
super-human; celestial being."
Source: Wikipedia

I was speechless. It was becoming ever more difficult to explain
away what I was seeing and hearing. Try as I might, I couldn't
escape the possibility that I was being introduced to a spirit
guide; a Mandarin gentleman of reasonably tall stature for a
Chinese, with a long twirling moustache and an ornate garment
resembling a red and gold brocade dress that flares out from the
hips in a bell shape. Xian has the gravitas of an elder although
his appearance is younger than I would expect. His persona is
calm, wise and strong but he does have a wry humour when
circumstances permit him to show it. Not so long ago I was
sitting in our kitchen feeling very sorry for myself. The children
were being difficult, as children can be, I was tired, and Darius
and I were snapping at each other. I had so hoped for a calm
start to the day and instead it felt as if World War Three were
commencing in our home. I sat with my coffee, feeling depressed.
"Xian," I asked, "please can you help me? I just don't have the
energy to deal with this today." I immediately felt tingling
down the sides of my body; a sensation I have come to know as
a clear indication that Spirit are near. It became more and more
intense and as I looked up I saw Xian himself, standing large
as life in my kitchen in his familiar red and gold brocade. I was
so taken aback; I had often seen him in my mind's eye, on my
"screen", but never standing in front of me before. The room
took on a feeling of immense calm and reassurance and I knew
that I would be able to face the day. I had had a random selection
of music playing and just as Xian's image faded the device
suddenly switched to playing *Help* by the Beatles. This made me
smile; not only had Xian come to my aid when I asked him, he
had also provided a moment of light relief just when I needed

it the most. It also gave me a gentle nudge and reminded me not to take myself, or my circumstances, so seriously. Similarly, on the day on which I completed the manuscript for this book I was sitting in a local café, where I had escaped to write while Darius managed the children at home. After countless rewrites and edits I came finally to the point at which I felt my story was complete and that I could write no more. I felt a sense of calm achievement tinged with mental exhaustion and a slight sadness at coming to the end of such a fantastic adventure as writing a book. I sent out a thank you to Xian for being by my side as I wrote and felt the familiar tingling down both sides of my body that always accompanies his presence. Background music was playing in the café and at that precise moment began the Irving Berlin song, *Cheek to Cheek,* which repeats the refrain, "Heaven/ I'm in heaven". I took this as a reply from Xian, who clearly has a penchant for music. I am thrilled to know him and as I write I am beginning to feel his presence more often in my daily life.

Whether or not you find yourself having to suspend your disbelief when talking about spirit guides nobody can deny that the idea of a constant unseen companion is a reassuring one. I choose to believe that Xian was a very real earthly being whose path is now to guide me in my spiritual development. It's not just a case of having some kind of magic genie either; I know, from my experience and that of others, that we all have spirit guides but that they are not to be conjured for personal gain. I would never dream, for example, of asking Xian for winning lottery numbers, or even for other personal information about my future, such as whether any of my children will marry. I do not believe that we are meant to know this information, just as I believe that I was not meant to know about Romy's passing before it happened. The reason we choose our life situations is in order to learn, and if we cut the corners, chicken out or cheat the system then the only person we have cheated is ourself as we have denied ourselves that learning. The knowledge of Spirit, when it is given to those of us very much on the earth plane, is for the highest good: of ourselves, of others, and of the earth, and never for any other reason. Though sometimes, when the children are running riot and I can't find my keys I do ask Spirit to give me a clue as to their whereabouts and they don't seem to have a problem obliging.

Prompt: Now we are nearing the end of this book, has any of what you've read changed your perception? Look back at your answers to the questions about truth and now answer them, honestly, again.

Chapter 15

Remembering Your Own Story

We must be willing to get rid of the life we've planned, so as to have the life that is waiting for us.
– Joseph Campbell

The mythologist and writer Joseph Campbell, author of *The Hero with a Thousand Faces*, knew that we had to practise the art of letting go in order to find our path to our truth. I, and others before me, have suggested that we map out our life before we come here. However, once we arrive and grow to maturity, we begin to feel that we must put in place an altogether different plan for ourselves: study, commit to a certain profession, marry, have children, retire. Sometimes this plan has been the construct of others in our lives: parents, teachers or authority figures whose experience we trust and whom we believe know better than us how our life should pan out. What if the reality is that *we already know*? If we throw all the plans we make on earth out of the window, we are left with our inner truth, our knowing, which links us back to the plan we made before we came here – the "life that is waiting for us". All that we need to do is step out of our own way, and trust the path ahead.

In Tarot, the hero setting out on the journey is depicted as The Fool. Rather than representing a literal sense of that title, I have always thought of The Fool as carefree and light, carrying very little and keeping in mind the various directions and opportunities that life has to offer. I see in that depiction an individual whose mind is open, who is ready to trust his intuition and move forwards in his life with trust and optimism. I tend to use Tarot as a tool to connect with Spirit and do not profess to have an in-depth knowledge of the cards or the plethora of meanings behind them. When I read Tarot for a client, I tell a story from the pictures that present themselves to me on the cards and it ultimately falls to that individual to write his or her own story. Again in the words of Joseph Campbell, who shares a birthday – 26th March – with Romy: "Every story you tell is your own story." Whatever we write for ourselves, if we own it and commit to fully living this truth then it cannot fail us. However, placing the first step on this path is often difficult as we fall prey to negativity and doubt from ourselves and sometimes those around us.

Despite having spent many years sitting in development circles and taking courses and workshops with a variety of experienced mediums for a long time I felt that I was a beginner, with nothing to offer. The world of mediumship can be tough: it's critical enough from the "outside", where there exist many people who just do not believe what we believe and even more who wish to debunk it as lies or fraudulent activity. I respect anyone's view, and I will never argue with someone's beliefs. If phrased and offered in the right way, guidance from a medium or psychic can offer hope, lift our spirits and set us on a more purposeful path in life. It may also give us permission to revert to "writing our own story", to remember the plan we set out for ourselves in order to access the learning in this lifetime. I truly believe that listening to Spirit through a good medium or psychic and using our own awareness may help us to take ownership of our life's direction and begin to live in the way that we feel we always intended.

Attitudes such as those I describe above initially put me off using my abilities professionally but I know that I have spent much time and energy developing the abilities I was born with to the extent that I can use them to offer others guidance, advice and hope. If I spend time worrying about what others may think of me or my work, I lose time in helping those people. As long as I doubted my abilities and my purpose I found that life had a way of putting people and opportunities in my way to test my theories and drop some pretty big hints as to what it was I was supposed to be doing. It took me a very long time to trust any of these directions from Spirit, as I like to believe they were. You know those times when you face what seems like a big challenge and then you look back afterwards and everything seems so obvious? I've had many of those, but I used to brush them off or ignore them. Now, I see them as big flashing neon signs pointing me away from whatever distraction my life is presenting me with and nudging me back to my purpose.

Some years ago, while working as a reflexologist and a birth doula in the London clinic of Dr Gowri Motha I built up a small circle of clients. Some of these women were in the public eye, or celebrities. Sometimes I would visit these ladies' homes to give them reflexology and one or two of them befriended me. One morning, while visiting one of these clients – Joanna Berryman, at that time the wife of Guy Berryman, the bassist with Coldplay – we were chatting and I happened to let slip that I read Tarot. She immediately asked me whether I would consider working at her baby shower a couple of weeks from then, to give reflexology treatments and Tarot readings to her friends. I said yes straightaway to the reflexology but felt very nervous about the Tarot part. I explained to her that I wasn't "professional", that I had only done this for friends over the years and that I was very worried that my sitters might misinterpret what I was telling them. Additionally, I was anxious that offering Tarot in this kind of setting was somehow disrespectful to Spirit. I didn't want to be a circus sideshow, the fortune-teller throwing out clichéd statements for everyone to giggle about afterwards downstairs. Basically, I wasn't confident at all in my abilities and in the end only reluctantly agreed to go ahead on the proviso that Jo explained very clearly to her friends that my readings would be short and, while not to be taken as literal advice, were also not to be taken too lightly.

A couple of weeks later I was sitting upstairs in Jo's house while Guy and his bandmates messed about with instruments downstairs before her friends all arrived for the baby shower. This in itself was a surreal experience. The synchronicity of meeting and getting to know Jo has never been lost on me. As you may recall, the first song I ever listened to with Darius was Coldplay's *The Scientist*, which became "our song". While planning Romy's remembrance ceremony we listened to a lot of music, trying to find lyrics that felt appropriate while also being spiritually uplifting. At some point, I started playing *The Scientist* and as we listened to the lyrics they seemed to take on a new meaning for us both. This was one of the songs we played for Romy and it is fitting that we did. Back in 2006 it was a pretty cool moment in my life to be sitting upstairs in a house belonging to one of those musicians, listening while they played.

A while later, guests started to arrive for the baby shower and I prepared my reflexology chair upstairs ready to work. To my surprise, my first customer, the PA to the band, wanted a Tarot reading. This went well. For the record, client confidentiality means that I can never share details of sittings with anyone, and certainly not in a book unless they are agreed in advance or anonymous. As the afternoon unfolded I gave sitting after sitting. Reading the Tarot cards gave me a springboard in to tuning into Spirit and before long I was in full flow, connecting with ease to spirit communicators and passing on information and advice to my sitters. Not a single person asked for a reflexology session, and as one guest went downstairs and revealed the accuracy of what I had told her, another would come racing upstairs for a reading for herself. I have to admit I was stunned. This was the first time I had given sittings to anyone outside my immediate circle. These women were all strangers to me, added to which I was seeing them in such quick succession that it felt like a whirlwind, yet still I was somehow managing to give them information they found both accurate and helpful. My second surreal moment of the day occurred when, in the middle of a reading, the door to the room opened and a voice said, "Oh I'm so sorry! I was just looking for the bathroom." The owner of the voice was a major Hollywood film star who happened to be a friend of Jo's.

Looking back, I was a total novice and really didn't handle my energy well. I didn't want to disappoint or let anyone down and, mindful of the fact that Jo was paying for my services for the afternoon, I wanted to make sure she felt she had her money's worth. This was ridiculous of me because she couldn't have been kinder or more gracious. The real test came towards the end of the afternoon as Jo's friend Kate, who had organised the shower, brought my final client for the day. I tried to keep my composure as a member of a world-famous girl band walked through the door. To be honest, any thoughts of being star-struck were superseded by sheer panic. How on earth could I give any kind of reading to this woman? Aside from the fact that she was all over major international newspapers and magazines on a regular basis, meaning that I "knew" all manner of things about her and her life, the sheer level of her fame would surely mean that she'd be closed and unreceptive. I have discovered that I much prefer knowing as little as possible about a client as this then presents me with a puzzle to solve. I also know that any information I do receive accurately, I can trust, as I know that I know nothing about the individual sitting in front of me. If I can't question it with my logical mind due to lack of information, I have to trust it – and this gives me more confidence to deliver a clear and helpful message. Nevertheless, this was Jo's friend, world famous singer or not, and she was sitting across from me waiting expectantly. I took a deep breath, asked her to shuffle the cards, and began.

To begin with, all my fears were realised as I tentatively gave snippets of information. As I suspected, her fame had served to make her a little reserved. I could tell that she was a warm, funny and friendly woman but that she had no intention of letting her guard down. Her energy felt closed and distant in a polite but firm way and it was making it all the more difficult for me to connect with her. I offered her one or two pieces of information that she politely batted away. I felt my spirits sink. On top of the fact that I had worked for several hours straight, such had been my desperation to do a good job that I hadn't even accepted my host's invitation to go downstairs and join the rest of the party for food and drink. I was hungry, my energy levels were low and my head was spinning. I hadn't taken proper care of myself and now I had the ultimate test – a celebrity client with high expectations – and I wasn't going to be able to deliver. I felt myself beginning to panic and inwardly begged Spirit for some help in getting myself out of the foolish situation I found myself in.

I immediately recalled something Gerrie had always taught us when we practised giving sittings in class. If you don't know: always be honest. No one is for everyone, and if for some reason (usually one that seems inexplicable at the time but then makes sense later) you're not getting it right for a sitter, don't waste their time. Simply be honest, tell them, and send them on their way. I took a deep breath and prepared myself to say something like, "Look, I'm really sorry but I'm tired and nervous. Obviously I'm aware of who you are, and because of that I also think I know various things about you and I'm afraid that I won't be able to give you an accurate or helpful sitting. I'm so sorry but I have to stop today." As I opened my mouth to speak, my eye caught a detail on one of the cards, and as it did, I felt myself tune into Spirit. I instantly saw an image on the "cinema screen" behind my eyes and it was so clear and so obvious that instead of giving the speech I'd prepared, I gave the information; something to do with a plan she had for a future direction for her career which was completely unrelated to her current one. In one fell swoop, the energy changed. The singer's face rearranged its pleasant, guarded look to one of utter astonishment. "Oh my goodness!" she exclaimed. "That's incredible! That's absolutely correct but it's something I've been thinking over and I haven't told a single soul about my plans yet. How did you know that?" From that moment, it was as if a curtain had fallen away and the information came thick and fast. I could hardly keep up, and by the end of half an hour I was on the floor. My client returned downstairs and I could hear her telling the others, "She's a mind reader! I've never experienced anything like it!"

My euphoria was soon overshadowed by utter exhaustion and I reproached myself for being so foolish. I had learned several important lessons that afternoon and resolved that, if I were to continue working, then I had to rethink my structure. I also saw that, despite my own opinion of myself as a "novice medium" with nothing of any value to share, I had been well and truly put on the spot by Spirit and I had delivered. You can't get much more obvious a confidence boost than fifteen or twenty satisfied clients in one afternoon.

Once I became embroiled in the chaotic business of a growing family, I placed my focus on my reflexology and doula work and set up a small but successful business that I managed to run around my mothering commitments. Mediumship, Tarot and that part of my life began to recede into a distant memory. I was so occupied with running a house, looking after two children under the age of two and attempting to set up my business that I just didn't have the space or the energy to give to my work with Spirit. Our welcoming and friendly fellow villagers were slightly less esoteric in their values and beliefs than we were, and I instinctively felt that setting up shop as a medium might have ruffled a few feathers or, at the very least, marked me out as more of an outsider than I already felt.

Today, we live in Brighton: a seaside resort, part of the city of Brighton and Hove and just half an hour from where we once lived. Known for its diversity and acceptance of all things alternative, it provides the perfect setting for me to return to my psychic studies and to research and write on the subject. Even this was revealed to me by Spirit many years ago. Shortly before Darius came into my life I had been single for a while and felt myself leaning towards a career change: from managing public relations for Battersea Dogs & Cats Home to reflexology and healing. I made several trips from London to Brighton by train just to walk around and absorb the surroundings. I never knew why I felt such a pull to Brighton, but it was drawing me to it. After I met Darius events unfolded and we remained in London, but Brighton still had a place in my heart. When Kasper was five months old Darius and I visited to celebrate an anniversary and then made one or two consecutive trips to see whether we could envisage ourselves living there. We didn't think we could.

One evening late in 2009 Darius returned home from work to be met by me declaring, "Let's move to Sussex!" He remained typically impassive and asked me what had prompted this inspired decision and my answer was, "I don't know but I just think we should live there." Despite having no family in the near vicinity and no connections to the area, Spirit had been giving me persistent signals and I couldn't ignore them any longer. Within a few weeks we were packing up our small London flat and heading for a new life in a Sussex village. When we landed properly in Brighton in June 2015 I knew that I had been destined to live there all along.

After all that I have experienced in my life to date, all the pathways I have trodden, all the things I tried and failed at and all the events that at the time seemed unfair, my truth was right in front of me. It was inside me; I knew it. When I look back at my story now, it all seems so obvious. Writing was always there. Teaching, and speaking, were always there. Communicating with Spirit was always there. In fact, communicating with Spirit was just something I always did in my daily life; chatting away with my granddad or various spirits and guides. The times of my life when I stopped chatting with Spirit were the times when things became confusing, difficult and out of control.

It has taken me four decades to rediscover my truth but now that I am in it and living it, my life feels very different and when I listen to my gut, my intuition, to Spirit, or to all or any of these combinations, the necessary things fall into place to enable me to move forwards. If things seem to take a turn different from the outcome I've been expecting, I no longer allow myself to feel disappointment. Okay, sometimes I do feel a little disappointment, but I give myself a short period of time to "grieve my loss" and then focus on what I need to learn from the experience. I also ask myself, "What am I missing here?" "What can I do differently?" Once I move forwards from that point, I always reach the best outcome for me at that time.

A great example of this is how this book came to be published. It was a childhood dream of mine to be a published author. I knew that I had a talent for writing but I allowed conventional opinion to persuade me that pursuing this wasn't a "proper" job. If I had thought more creatively about the issue I might have come up with some solutions involving part-time work which paid my bills and gave me an opportunity to hone my skills, but I chose instead to listen to what I thought was sense.

After Romy died, I was in the frustrating position of being unable to work due to my depression, PTSD, and the simple fact that grief prevents some of us from functioning in a useful way. My memory was shot, I was still having distressing flashbacks and I was in shock. I was in no fit state to commit to anything before I healed myself. In this position, and being someone whose energy commands me to "do" rather than just "be" (not great for meditation!), I found myself tinkering with writing for the first time since my adolescence. As I gained in confidence through the compliments I received on my blog, I began to write down thoughts that I felt would collate together into a book. At that point, I had no idea what the structure or message of the book would be, but I knew that Romy was at the centre of it. Slowly, it began to evolve into a collection of my experiences with Spirit over the years, rounded off with what I hoped would be inspirational springboards to discussion, or "prompts" at the end of each chapter. I wondered how my book might be able to offer help to others by giving them an insight into what, for me, had served me well as a normal way of life.

It was around this time that a number of events all unfolded around me at the exact same time, leading me to draw the conclusion that my book was going to be published by a major mind, body, spirit publisher. I attended a workshop with an attached competition to win a publishing contract. The deadline date for submissions was Romy's birthday, 26th March. This was a sign. I felt that I could win. In fact, I began to believe strongly that my book was going to be published.

Having a deadline date was essential for me as my free time outside of caring for the children was limited to non-existent. When Macsen slept for up to two hours after lunch each day, this became my writing time. It was really hard. On some days, he woke up and needed settling so I ended up typing one-handed while breastfeeding. In the online writers' forum from the workshop, I read that others were travelling abroad for writing sabbaticals, taking time off work, reading inspirational books on releasing creative block and the like and I started to panic. All I seemed to be doing was changing nappies, making packed lunches, wiping – floors, surfaces, noses and bottoms – and typing 200 words at a time with one hand. Getting up early was impossible as Macsen still slept with us and the slightest movement at that time in the morning would wake him up. Come evening, I was so exhausted from the day that getting my best work out of me was a total non-starter. As 26th March rolled around I managed, with backup from Darius and my parents, to complete and submit a proposal and chapters that I felt happy with. Guess what? I didn't win.

When the announcement of the winner came, I'll admit that I pulled the car over on the way to pick up the children from school, and I cried. For about half an hour, the sense of despair I felt was so strong I began to doubt whether it had been a good idea to start this process after all. The negative voice in my head was telling me that I was a complete and utter failure and urging me to throw in the towel for good and forget this writing business because I couldn't do it. On top of this, I couldn't understand how my psychic abilities had let me down. I had had a clear sign that I was meant to win this competition. Maybe it was all nonsense after all.

I allowed myself an hour or two to wallow and then I dusted myself down, called Michelle and Emma and told them how disappointed I felt. Emma told me at once, "This just isn't the right publisher at the right time for you." And Michelle pointed out that, for all the best sporting champions, there is always one big loss that redefines them and makes them get their head down and go on to the success they have worked for. I thought about these pieces of advice very carefully. Emma was right. The more I thought about the publisher I'd approached, the more I could appreciate that perhaps we weren't the perfect fit for each other after all. I admired them and many of their authors greatly but I was a little uncomfortable with the sheer enormity of their operation. I wondered how freely I would tell my story had I been distracted by the expectations of the publicity machine and inevitable comparisons (mainly by myself) to other, established professional mediums. I dug out an email from my friend Theresa, a successful author and woman of extraordinary generosity of spirit. Despite never having met me in person she has mentored me ever since I contacted her in 2014 to tell her that I had found one of her books of immense help after Romy died. Theresa had emailed me to suggest that I contact O-Books, a dedicated mind, body, spirit publishing imprint. I went back to my proposal, tweaked some parts, added in three more chapters

– which came remarkably easily – and sent everything off. Two weeks later, I had a book deal.

The point of this story is this: I have always had a knowing that I could, and would, write a book that would be published. Having to organise myself to the deadline of that writing competition was crucial, as without it, I would doubtless still be one of those people who are perpetually "writing a book". At the time I write these words of course I have no idea where the story of this book will end but I believe strongly that it will reach those who will find something in it to be of help. I have known my whole life that it was my purpose to write, to heal and to teach, and I tried coming at this in a variety of different ways. I sidestepped it, I packaged it as something else, I ignored it and I told myself I just wasn't good enough at it. It took the birth, and passing, of my daughter Romy to bring me back to exactly why this was my purpose in the first place. Once again, in spite of my self-doubt, Spirit gave me a nudge and ensured that I was in the right place at the right time. Of course, they did not physically pick me up and put me there, but my years of looking and listening for direction and clues from Spirit automatically kicked in and almost without thinking I simply followed their lead. If you set the intention or ask the question and then relax and step aside, Spirit can show you the way. The truth was inside me all along, but I was so busy trying to "find myself" that I failed to see that it was all there right in front of me.

There exist many books in the world today about Finding Your Purpose, Following Your Path, Surviving After Trauma. There are shouty capitals and galvanising rants. I know because I have read many of them. Some have helped me; others have not. This book is on an altogether more delicate vibration but I hope that its message is clear and strong: look for Spirit in your life. Listen to Spirit. You don't have to look far because they are just in the next room looking out for you and helping you back to your path. Live your life safe in the knowledge that, ever since you were born, you have known exactly what it is that you came here to do. You plotted your route, including all the pitfalls and difficulties. You wanted to experience them all because you wanted to learn this lesson in a particular way, with particular people. You all agreed this together, even the experiences where one of you would cause pain to the other. This was agreed because this is how we learn and grow spiritually.

> *The spiritual journey is individual, highly personal. It can't be organised or regulated.*
>
> *It isn't true that everyone should follow one path. Listen to your own truth.*
> **– Ram Dass**

I recognised my truth through my daughter's existence – here on earth and in the afterlife. I hope that now, through revisiting your own story alongside mine – you find yours.

Prompt: Begin with writing down your own story, both historically and going forwards. This doesn't have to be an epic novel, it can be a series of short phrases, a flow diagram or a mood board. If you write your story in bite-sized chunks, your truth will begin to emerge or, if you find it's not easy to recognise your truth at this point, at the very least something of substance which could help you going forward in your life. What do you notice about it? Where were the points of greatest learning? How can you plot a path forwards from here?

References

I mention in this book several books that provide interesting further reading. For reference, I list them here with my thanks for all that they have illuminated for me:

Many Lives, Many Masters. Weiss, Dr Brian (Piatkus, 1988)

Other Lives, Other Selves: A Jungian Psychotherapist Discovers Past Lives. Woolger, Roger (Thorsons, 1999)

Spiritual Midwifery. Gaskin, Ina May (Book Publishing Company, 1975)

Spirit Babies. Makichen, Walter (Bantam Dell, 2005)

Answers from Heaven. Cheung and Broad (Piatkus, 2017)

Tell Me Your Truth

Thank you for purchasing, and taking the time to read, *The Truth Inside*. If what you have read in these pages speaks to you and you feel so inclined, please do leave a review on the website of your favourite online bookstore.

Please also visit my website: www.alinorell.com to sign up for my mailing list and "Like" my Facebook page, Ali Norell Author, to be kept informed well ahead of time of any future books.

I always have several book ideas bubbling away at any one time and welcome correspondence with my readers as well as any input in the form of stories. Has reading this book helped you to see your life in a different way? Have you had your own encounters with Spirit? If you have stories to share, then I would love to hear them, particularly if you are a bereaved parent who has had communication from a child in Spirit. Please send them to ali@alinorell.com and you may find them in a future book (with your prior permission, of course).

If your life takes a new turn as a result of reading this book I would be thrilled to hear from you. Tell me your truth!

Author biography

Ali Norell is a mother – of three children here and one in Spirit – a wife, an author, a healer, a medium and an inspirational speaker.

Since early childhood Ali has been able to see, hear and sense the spirits of those who have passed and those who serve as guides from the spirit world. Following many and varied careers – including that of a tour guide taking coach tours across Europe and public relations manager for both Battersea Dogs & Cats Home and the Royal Botanic Gardens, Kew – she made a decision to follow a different path. She retrained and spent a decade working as a reflexologist specialising in fertility and pregnancy and combining this with work as a birth doula. She also trained and worked as a healer and spent many years developing skills as a spiritual medium, giving sittings to friends and colleagues and taking part in some platform demonstrations of mediumship.

Eventually her passion for Spiritualism began to take over and she decided that she wanted to begin her work with the "other end" of this life. This decision was cemented following the passing to Spirit of her youngest daughter, Romy, in July 2014. Ali's belief in an afterlife and the many communications she received from Romy after her passing eventually caused her to believe that she is meant to use her abilities to help others; especially those who grieve.

Ali's dearest wish is to help others to see that our loved ones are never "lost". They are right beside us, helping us and willing us on in our purpose.

Ali lives in Brighton, UK with her husband, three children and two cats.

BOOKS

O-BOOKS

SPIRITUALITY

O is a symbol of the world, of oneness and unity; this eye represents knowledge and insight. We publish titles on general spirituality and living a spiritual life. We aim to inform and help you on your own journey in this life.

If you have enjoyed this book, why not tell other readers by posting a review on your preferred book site? Recent bestsellers from O-Books are:

Heart of Tantric Sex
Diana Richardson
Revealing Eastern secrets of deep love and intimacy to Western couples.
Paperback: 978-1-90381-637-0 ebook: 978-1-84694-637-0

Crystal Prescriptions
The A-Z guide to over 1,200 symptoms and their healing crystals
Judy Hall
The first in the popular series of six books, this handy little guide is packed as tight as a pill-bottle with crystal remedies for ailments.
Paperback: 978-1-90504-740-6 ebook: 978-1-84694-629-5

Take Me To Truth
Undoing the Ego
Nouk Sanchez, Tomas Vieira
The best-selling step-by-step book on shedding the Ego, using the teachings of *A Course In Miracles*.
Paperback: 978-1-84694-050-7 ebook: 978-1-84694-654-7

The 7 Myths about Love...Actually!
The journey from your HEAD to the HEART of your SOUL
Mike George
Smashes all the myths about LOVE.
Paperback: 978-1-84694-288-4 ebook: 978-1-84694-682-0

The Holy Spirit's Interpretation of the New Testament
A course in Understanding and Acceptance
Regina Dawn Akers
Following on from the strength of *A Course In Miracles*, NTI teaches us how to experience the love and oneness of God.
Paperback: 978-1-84694-085-9 ebook: 978-1-78099-083-5

The Message of A Course In Miracles
A translation of the text in plain language
Elizabeth A. Cronkhite
A translation of *A Course in Miracles* into plain, everyday language for anyone seeking inner peace. The companion volume, *Practicing A Course In Miracles*, offers practical lessons and mentoring.
Paperback: 978-1-84694-319-5 ebook: 978-1-84694-642-4

Thinker's Guide to God
Peter Vardy
An introduction to key issues in the philosophy of religion.
Paperback: 978-1-90381-622-6

Your Simple Path
Find happiness in every step
Ian Tucker
A guide to helping us reconnect with what is really important in
our lives.
Paperback: 978-1-78279-349-6 ebook: 978-1-78279-348-9

365 Days of Wisdom
Daily Messages To Inspire You Through The Year
Dadi Janki
Daily messages which cool the mind, warm the heart and guide
you along your journey.
Paperback: 978-1-84694-863-3 ebook: 978-1-84694-864-0

Body of Wisdom
Women's Spiritual Power and How it Serves
Hilary Hart
Bringing together the dreams and experiences of women across
the world with today's most visionary spiritual teachers.
Paperback: 978-1-78099-696-7 ebook: 978-1-78099-695-0

Dying to Be Free
From Enforced Secrecy to Near Death to True Transformation
Hannah Robinson
After an unexpected accident and near-death experience, Hannah
Robinson found herself radically transforming her life, while a
remarkable new insight altered her relationship with her father, a
practising Catholic priest.
Paperback: 978-1-78535-254-6 ebook: 978-1-78535-255-3

The Ecology of the Soul
A Manual of Peace, Power and Personal Growth for Real People
in the Real World
Aidan Walker
Balance your own inner Ecology of the Soul to regain your
natural state of peace, power and wellbeing.
Paperback: 978-1-78279-850-7 ebook: 978-1-78279-849-1

Practicing A Course In Miracles
A Translation of the Workbook in Plain Language and With
Mentoring Notes
Elizabeth A. Cronkhite
The practical second and third volumes of The Plain-Language
A Course In Miracles.
Paperback: 978-1-84694-403-1 ebook: 978-1-78099-072-9

Quantum Bliss
The Quantum Mechanics of Happiness, Abundance, and Health
George S. Mentz
Quantum Bliss is the breakthrough summary of success and
spirituality secrets that customers have been waiting for.
Paperback: 978-1-78535-203-4 ebook: 978-1-78535-204-1

Readers of ebooks can buy or view any of these bestsellers by
clicking on the live link in the title. Most titles are published
in paperback and as an ebook. Paperbacks are available in
traditional bookshops. Both print and ebook formats are
available online.

Find more titles and sign up to our readers' newsletter at
http://www.johnhuntpublishing.com/mind-body-spirit

Follow us on Facebook at https://www.facebook.com/OBooks/
and Twitter at https://twitter.com/obooks